Seasons
of the Spirit

Text copyright © Teresa Morgan 2010
The author asserts the moral right
to be identified as the author of this work

Published by
The Bible Reading Fellowship
15 The Chambers, Vineyard
Abingdon OX14 3FE
United Kingdom
Tel: +44 (0)1865 319700
Email: enquiries@brf.org.uk
Website: www.brf.org.uk
BRF is a registered charity

ISBN 978 1 84101 710 5

First published 2010
10 9 8 7 6 5 4 3 2 1 0
All rights reserved

Acknowledgments
Unless otherwise stated, scripture quotations are taken from the New Revised Standard
Version of the Bible, copyright © 1989, 1995 by the Division of Christian Education of the
National Council of the Churches of Christ in the United States of America, and are used by
permission. All rights reserved.

Scripture quotations taken from the Revised Standard Version of the Bible, copyright © 1946,
1952, 1971 by the Division of Christian Education of the National Council of the Churches of
Christ in the United States of America, are used by permission. All rights reserved.

Extracts from the Authorised Version of the Bible (The King James Bible), the rights in which
are vested in the Crown, are reproduced by permission of the Crown's Patentee, Cambridge
University Press

Extracts from The Book of Common Prayer of 1662, the rights of which are vested in the
Crown in perpetuity within the United Kingdom, are reproduced by permission of Cambridge
University Press, Her Majesty's Printers.

Extract from the Covenant Service taken from *The Methodist Worship Book* © 1999 Trustees for
Methodist Church Purposes. Used with permission.

A catalogue record for this book is available from the British Library

Printed in Singapore by Craft Print International Ltd

Seasons
of the Spirit

*One community's journey
through the Christian year*

Teresa Morgan

To the congregation of St Mary and St Nicholas, Littlemore

Contents

Foreword

Teresa Morgan has a delightful way of writing. She draws you in to the world of everyday things in an Anglican parish where the normal events of people's lives weave their way through the rhythm of the year. She observes the depth in ordinary things and the original texture in the mundane.

It's hard to define this writing too closely. In part it's one priest's reflections on the round of the year. In part it's a series of poetic musings. In part it's classic Anglican pastoral theology, taking seriously (but not solemnly) the small realities of life and exploring their significance. As Teresa says herself, 'Fragments of other people's lives prise my imagination open like a tin.' Then off we go exploring.

However this writing is described, it's rich. Teresa writes fluently, with the sharp observation of a student of life who seeks to relate what she sees and experiences to the God she glimpses round the corner of everything. She starts with an observation in which you recognise a forgotten thought—'There is something satisfying about a really gloomy December…'—and within a few sentences you find yourself pondering the doubts John the Baptist had about whether Jesus really was 'the one who is to come'. We start with the writer going to take an early service because the vicar has gone to Cardiff to watch Wales play rugby, and soon we find ourselves deep in the power of religious stories: 'They are the way we converse with the cosmos.' This is surely the writing of one whose God and King has taught her 'in all things thee to see'.

Above all, Teresa celebrates 'the importance of unspectacular lives'. This is truly faithful ministry, recognising the density in the detail. After a funeral she writes of those she buries, 'The glimpses I get of them through their family and friends fill me with wonder.' She reminds us that local saints are important because, like family, we're stuck with them, but then we can discover their deep, hidden qualities. This is a true pastoral instinct. In a culture obsessed with celebrity, it's hard to get across the truth that no lives are boring; they're just undiscovered.

I commend this book warmly. It's wise and generous; it's accessible and full of insight; it refreshes the soul. Readers will come to these pages and be strangely entranced.

+John Pritchard
Bishop of Oxford

Prologue: Remembrance

It is six o'clock on Remembrance Sunday: my annual visit to the British Legion. I thread the back streets of Littlemore in a fine rain. Street lamps smoulder darkly. Behind them, buildings swim in and out of focus: sheltered accommodation, council houses, low-rise flats. The occasional pedestrian is a bowed silhouette. The local shops are silent, their steel blinds lowered and locked.

The Legion looks like a relic of the war, a squat, square bunker fortified by a wire fence. Inside it is cosy and noisy, more social club than military outpost. I change into cassock and surplice in the office behind the bar, pinning a smart silk poppy to my preaching scarf. Club members of all ages are already seated round the edges of the lounge, whiskies and pints before them on small tables. The elderly are wearing their campaign medals. The young look bored, their parents adamant. Conversation filters in from the games room opposite; a thwack of darts and occasional applause.

We lay two standards on a drum-head altar while Jubilee Brass plays 'O God, our help in ages past'. In the past, the air used to be thick with cigarette smoke—soldiers' incense—bearing our act of remembrance to heaven. I find myself perversely missing it today. The service has a disorganised dignity, casual but heartfelt. Among those here tonight are descendants of men who died in the Boer war, two World Wars and the Falklands—more distant conflicts too, no doubt, which we have forgotten.

We hear part of John 15: 'Greater love hath no man than this…'. I reflect that there is something Christ-like about men and women who lay down their lives for their friends.

What is less often noticed is that there is also something divine about remembering. Human beings are so very afraid of oblivion. To forget, we feel, is to lose what we have forgotten. If we forget enough, we lose ourselves, and others who forget are lost to us. And to be 'lost' is another word for being parted from God. But since it is unbearable to think we could be lost to God, we put our faith in God's good memory. In God, we trust, nothing and no one is lost; no one is overlooked, no one forgotten.

This will be the first year within my memory that the words of remembrance are not spoken by Jim. We lose one of our veterans every year, now. The brave declaration sounds in my ears like a plea. Do not let us forget, Lord, as we grow old and our dead slip further from us. Do not let the busyness of living overtake us till we no longer have time or energy to remember those we have lost, those who lost us, who lost everything for us. Help us to pass on the torch: to touch the imaginations of the young so that what we experienced does not die with us.

The Reveille wakes us from our individual musings and the band leads us in a rousing rendition of 'O valiant hearts'.

The parish of Littlemore, on the south-eastern edge of Oxford, bound to the city and barred from it by the ringroad, is still essentially a village. Its heart is medieval, too young to appear in the Domesday Book but mentioned in the twelfth century as 'Luthlemoria', 'little marsh'. A few ancient stone houses survive among a handful of Victorian brick villas but Littlemore's origins are shrouded in forgetting—as, already, are the beginnings of my relationship with it.

I seem to remember my first visit quite clearly. It was Palm Sunday and I walked in halfway through the service, having forgotten that it began at ten o'clock. But I must be wrong, because Palm Sunday is the one day of the year when the service begins at eleven. Anyway, that wasn't my first visit. The previous Advent, the vicar had recruited me to form part of a string quartet at the community carol service. Even that wasn't really the beginning because, when my sister and I were children, our parents brought us to church and afterwards to lunch with the then vicar, David Nicholls, and his wife Gilly. She was (and is) a doctor, he an authority on the Caribbean, and they kept a macaw called Archdeacon Paley, who wrote controversial letters to *The Times*. Members of the congregation who are now friends must have been present on each of those occasions but, if I asked now, who would remember? Services overlie each other in the mind year after year, until they are stuck together like old photographs.

Growing up in those days in North Oxford, I knew almost nothing about this side of town. My mental map of the city featured the Woodstock and Banbury Roads, schools and shops and the houses of friends, the colleges where my parents worked, and an eclectic range of places of worship. Under the influence of our father, a theologian by profession and a non-stipendiary priest, Catharine and I attended the local parish church and sang in the church choir. Under the aegis of our mother, who taught the study of religions, we attended Catholic masses and Quaker meetings, and visited synagogues, mosques, gurdwaras, temples and meditation centres. It was a stimulating combination—though, for my parents, their different approaches to religion proved to be one of many incompatibilities and they parted company while we were still children.

When, years later, I came back to Oxford to work, I bought a house on the south-east side of town, and looked for a new parish church to attend. My father, now vicar of Sandford-on-Thames, recommended neighbouring Littlemore and its clergy: a New Testament scholar, John Muddiman, and a musician, Bernhard Schünemann. 'You'll like them,' he said; 'you'll learn from them.' It proved good advice. There have been other beginnings since, all equally buried in my reliable amnesia for the prime moment: my first sermon, ordination, first celebration of the Eucharist… However hard we try, we forget far more than we remember.

In the days when many clergy stayed in one parish for decades, one of their functions was to remember. They remembered the parents and grandparents of current congregations; the distant cousins; who had been whose friend or enemy. They remembered baptising and marrying many of those whom they buried; they knew who had come to the village as a bride, whose uncle had emigrated and whose grandfather had been killed in war. It all helped to hold the community together. At the moment, in a village like Littlemore, many members of the congregation have longer memories than the clergy—but that too is changing as everyone moves around more. When the present generation has passed away, I wonder whether anyone will be able to look back more than a few years. It is just one of many challenges the parish faces.

Still, I reflect, as I disrobe and stow my poppy carefully away for another year, it is also important to make the most of the present and look forward to the future. I am grateful to be in Littlemore now, playing my small role in the parish and keeping Remembrance Sunday in good company. The band strikes up a dance tune as I let myself out. I cycle home down the Iffley Road against the wind, which means it's winter. In summer the wind rebuffs you as you cycle up the hill; in winter it's in your favour. The estates round here have beautiful names: Rose Hill, Blackbird Leys, Minchery Farm. Reality is less idyllic but equally colourful.

Advent Sunday

What are we waiting for? December
dim as church glass; the vase
of my temple dry and flowers
withered. What are we waiting for?
Trees stripped of oracles and grass
bated with ice.

Ask the robin what he knows
to stoke his beacon.
Hollies butting through the hedge
and swaggering mistletoe have their reasons.
What light knocks
where the horizon lifts its lid
and our sky shell is thinnest?

Suns spin like a sovereign down:
will it be soon or late?
Life crouches at the tips of twigs:
make haste.

John the Baptist

There is something satisfying about a really gloomy December; it makes Christmas shine more brightly. Today is doleful enough even for me. Bulging grey skies drizzle greyly on gleaming grey roads. The celebrant borrows my chasuble, which is too small for him but, being made of thick William Morris curtain material, is the warmest we have. It's the third Sunday of Advent, when we celebrate John the Baptist, if 'celebrate' is the right word. Not, perhaps, the most sympathetic character in the Advent story (where he's a bit of an interloper anyway). He's an extremist. When crowds of people come to him to be baptised, he calls them a brood of vipers and accuses them of not being really sorry.

John strikes me as a lonely figure, standing as he does between the old and new covenants. Like the prophets before him, he doesn't like his world, but neither is he destined to change it. He isn't the one for whom everyone is waiting. He is the first man to acknowledge Christ as an adult and, in his lifetime, no one comes closer to understanding Jesus' mission, but he dies without seeing the results of what he helped to start. He preaches repentance and baptism and looks for the coming of the kingdom, but he is never part of Jesus' circle of close friends.

Despite his rebarbative manner, John also invites sympathy because, man of faith that he is, he also experiences doubt. From prison, he sends word to Jesus: 'Are you the one who is to come, or are we to wait for another?'[1] It seems extraordinary, when all the signs are that he knew Jesus as soon as he met him. Did he not understand some of the things Jesus was doing? Was his faith shaken by his own sufferings?

Whatever the reason, John's doubt reminds us that even the strongest people have moments of weakness—which is encouraging at this time of year, when many people feel oppressed by darkness and uncertainty. John knew that feeling but he also knew the words that he had borrowed from Isaiah: 'Prepare the way of the Lord; make straight in the desert a highway for our God. Every valley shall be lifted up, and every mountain and hill be made low; the uneven ground shall become level, and the rough places a plain. Then the glory of the Lord shall be revealed, and all people shall see it together.'[2]

Outside, after the service, the sky is practically hanging round our necks. The cedar at the north-western corner of the church looms blackly and drips on people as they emerge. I jump up and down to keep warm. 'You want to go inside,' people say, but I quite like it in the murk. Anyway, it isn't much warmer indoors: two of the heaters are broken and I'm sure the temperature is below the legal minimum for workplaces. (I suppose this doesn't apply to us, as no one counts as an employee here.) Ivy has saved the non-coffee drinker a cup of hot water. 'You get that down you, girl.'

On my way home, I cycle round to the Mobile Home Park to return a tape we used in a funeral last week. I love an excuse to come here—our own model village of miniature castles, set in formal gardens which in summer are brilliant with hanging baskets and bedding plants. The park is technically in Sandford parish and we buried the dead man in his family plot in Sandford churchyard, but, thanks to some feud long pre-dating the present incumbents, the family refused to step inside Sandford church, so the service was held at Littlemore. From one church to the other we processed behind Oxford's only horse-drawn hearse, a Gothic wonder of jet paintwork, gilt and plate glass, stuffed with yellow chrysanthemums and drawn by four plumed and polished geldings. Walking sedately in its wake over the railway and the dual carriageway, past fields from which ordinary brown and grey ponies gazed in envy, we felt almost Dickensian and, by association, inappropriately but irrepressibly Christmassy.

Fourth Sunday of Advent: the Virgin Mary

Littlemore church is dedicated to St Mary the Virgin, after its mother church, the University Church of Oxford, and to St Nicholas, patron of the nearby Mynchery, the medieval Benedictine nunnery. It is not an old parish, having been founded in the 1830s by John Henry Newman.

When he became vicar of the University Church in 1828, Newman discovered that Littlemore was part of his parish. Since it lay a good three miles from the centre of Oxford up a steep hill, this seemed to him impractical and he set about building it a chapel and a school, with a view to installing a curate there. His mother, who lived nearby on Rose Hill, laid the foundation stone. A plaque commemorates her on the north wall of the aisle: 'Sacred to the memory of Jemima Newman, who laid the first stone of this chapel, July 21st 1835; and died before it was finished, May 17th 1836, in the 64th year of her age.' The relief above it shows the angel Gabriel offering a crown to the Virgin Mary against a backdrop of the half-built church. Mary is looking in consternation at a pile of books, which she seems to have dropped when the angel spoke to her. Since, as Newman insisted, this is not an annunciation scene but some evidently later meeting, it seems odd that she looks so surprised.

Visitors do not find it a pretty church, though the chancel may have been designed by Pugin and there are several William Morris windows. It is small, cell-shaped and plain—nothing to compare with the Norman glory of Iffley or the Victorian temples of the Cowley Road. It is built of yellowish local stone, now rather blackened; a low tower to one side of the chancel houses a calling-bell and a charitably slow clock. Inside, the walls are whitewashed and damp. The east window is supposed to be rather fine and there is some grand Gothic painting in red, blue and gold behind the altar. Apart from Jemima's, the only monuments are war memorials and a brass plaque to David Nicholls, with the Archdeacon on his shoulder. A slender screen, plain pulpit and fixed pews, a wizard's-hat cover over a medieval font (out of the University Church), a boxy organ (out of the old psychiatric hospital) and a wooden statue of the Virgin Mary, on the wall opposite Jemima, about complete the decoration.

If you worship here for a while, it looks better and better. You begin to appreciate how perfectly the iron grilles fit into the floor (unlike in so many churches, where they rock and clang). You notice how beadlike strings of colour swing across the walls as the sun shines through the monastically narrow windows. The plain woodwork makes a fine backdrop for flowers. Churches are like people: you have to spend time with them, and then the plainest can be revealed as the most beautiful. Like Mary herself, perhaps—an unexceptional teenager who becomes more and more remarkable as we get to know her.

I preach on Mary as the new Abraham, mother of a new people. Mary's own song of praise links her with Abraham, but she is also very much herself: shrewd, joyful, courageous, humble, a woman who dares to bless the God who has blessed her. Paradoxically, part of being very much herself is that, like the patriarchs and prophets before her, she lets God work through her, so she becomes a blessing.

Letting oneself be used by God is one of the great challenges of spiritual life. Most of us have a fairly strong sense of who we are and how we'd like our lives to be. We want a certain kind of family or house or car or job; we want to have friends, to be successful or admired or loved. To give up our desires and let God use our lives in ways we might not have planned or wanted is both difficult and frightening. If God sent an angel to us with a life-changing proposition, would we follow Mary's example and say 'yes'?

Who can say? But it is encouraging that in the Bible, letting ourselves be used by God never means becoming less ourselves. If anything, holy men and women, from Abraham to Moses, Elijah to Esther to Jesus himself, are larger than life, more fully themselves than those around them. The Spirit does not blow our selves away; it blows through the shape of us, using our qualities and personalities for divine ends. Jesus says, 'Those who want to save their life will lose it, and those who lose their life for my sake, and for the sake of the gospel, will save it.'[3] Paul adds that 'there are varieties of gifts, but the same Spirit; there are varieties of services, but the same Lord; and there are varieties of activities, but it is the same God who activates all of them in everyone. To each is given the manifestation of the Spirit for the common good.'[4]

Mary's life-changing 'yes' to God—'Let it be with me according to your word'[5]—sets the agenda and poses the challenge of Advent. Come Christmas, we shall talk not only of the blessing God offers us but also of the blessing we give God and the blessing we hope to become for other people. It takes courage to let ourselves be used, but those who manage it—all generations call them blessed.

— ❧ —

Carol services

It is axiomatic that carol services bring people together, so we have plenty. The Advent carol service on Advent Sunday is followed by the St Nicholas' Day procession on 6 December, the ecumenical community carol service a week or so before Christmas, the Christingle service and the blessing of the crib, not to mention carol services for schools and retirement homes. Sometimes Sandford church choir puts on a seasonal oratorio, too. There is a primitive thrill about arriving in darkness and finding the church ablaze with light and buzzing with conversation.

At the community carol service, despite the presence of such local dignitaries as councillors, head teachers and scout leaders, the atmosphere is more music festival than liturgy. There may be contributions from any or, with luck, all of a school choir, a folk group, a gospel choir and a string quartet. Paul, local music teacher and showman extraordinary, teaches the congregation a four-part round which he has written for the occasion. His accompaniment shakes dust out of the roof carvings. During Bernhard's incumbency, the Christmas tree was decorated with red wooden apples and real candles. Now that Margreet is our vicar, it wears white bows. Churchwarden Sue lurks behind it with a fire extinguisher.

The head of the local Muslim girls' school joins us and reads the story of the annunciation from the Koran. When he's read it in English, he reads a section in Arabic. The congregation is very quiet, a little overawed. Is this religious dialogue or something more profound? We don't know where we're going with it, only that we like and respect each other.

This year we have a new contribution from a group of

Egyptian Copts who have been holding services in the church on Saturdays. What romance the name of Egypt evokes! The birthplace of monasticism; home of our oldest texts of the Gospels and some of our earliest hymns and liturgies; source of some of the most creative theology of the early Church. I point out to anyone who will listen that although it is distant in time and space, Egyptian monasticism is particularly close to us in spirit, having inspired British missionaries like David and Columba. Our Egyptian friends read a passage from the Bible and sing a hymn in Coptic, to a plangent eastern melody.

There is a dark side to our celebrations. In recent years, there has been trouble with teenagers in the village, vandalising cars, breaking windows and throwing stones at people in the street. Now some of the congregation no longer go out after dark, even to carol services or midnight mass on Christmas Eve.

The next day, I visit Mary in one of the group homes attached to the psychiatric hospital. Just beyond them, where the road curves round towards Sandford, is the bridge over the ringroad from which people occasionally attempt suicide. Mary jumped off it a couple of years ago and achieved not oblivion but only intensive care, where she remained for many months. Now she is out, she's hoping to come to church again, and she hasn't given up hope of reading Theology at Oxford. Carols from King's float out of her radio, sounding a long way off. The choristers sing a medieval carol about another Mary who was 'makeless'—mateless and matchless.[6] We make an altar out of a chair and share Communion sitting on the bed. The difference between aloneness and loneliness, between community and community care, hovers uneasily in the air between us.

Holding the baby

Much as I like Christmas, Christmas Eve often finds me slightly anxious. What can I say at the midnight service that will touch the annual attenders, ruddy and cheerful from the pub, but also speak to the regulars, for whom tonight is one stop on a long pilgrimage?

This year, I talk about the many ways a Messiah may come: tearing open the heavens; defeating Israel's enemies; surrounded by angels; speaking tenderly to Jerusalem. There are Messiahs who burn like a refiner's fire and Messiahs who feed their flock like a shepherd, Messiahs who cast down the mighty from their thrones and Messiahs who reign from the throne of David. One thing they all have in common is that they appear as adults. They have to: they are warriors and leaders. But tonight, an angel announces to a group of shepherds that the Messiah has come to them in the form of a baby. 'A *baby*?' they might have said. 'Israel's praying for salvation and you're sending a *baby*? Are you insane?'

Why *did* God send a baby? I reflect on what we can say about babies. Not much, at first, except that they need a lot of looking after. Pretty soon, though, their individuality begins to emerge. Some aspects of a child's character are born with it, while others are acquired. Some children learn to trust people, to be kind to others, and some don't. Some learn to value education, some money, some God, and some not even themselves. How a child develops depends a lot on the people around him or her, and so it must be with Jesus. He is born with astonishing gifts but the man—the Messiah—he grows up to be will lie somewhere in the mysterious alchemy of nature and environment.

So tonight we celebrate a God who, rather than sending his Messiah ready-made, asks us to look after a Messiah in the making—to take part in our own salvation. 'Here is my Son,' he says. 'He has it in him to save the world, but only if you help him. Make him welcome. Teach him what he needs to learn—love and trust, and joy and hope. You can do it. You have all those things in you, even if you don't always feel or recognise them. Let looking after the baby bring out the best in you. Then, when he grows up and calls you to hear his good news, you'll be ready.'

It's a responsibility—and, as with any responsibility, it's only when we step up to it that we find out what we're really made of; what divine qualities of love and faithfulness wait, unsought or unsuspected, to grow within us.

No one person has every virtue, so looking after a child is always a communal enterprise, and so is looking after a church or a village. Community is strongly in evidence at the Christmas lunch. Though Margreet and her husband Julian began it, this is a village, not a church event. The hall of John Henry Newman primary school is transformed with streamers and balloons into a festive dining room. Long tables are covered in crisp Christmas paper, and laden with crackers and crocks. Everyone contributes something. Turkeys arrive in state, by car, powerfully fragrant under foil. Puddings and pies are borne on trays, in baskets, from the four corners of the parish. Pounds of potatoes are roasted, carrots and sprouts boiled, in the school kitchen. Old and young, singles and families, strangers and friends melt into one big group. After lunch, there is bingo for those who are still awake, a raffle, Christmas carols accompanied by a scratch band and, for those who even now like to be up and doing, gossip and washing-up in the kitchen.

There is magic in community. When we say the liturgy, our

words catch fire from words spoken around us. We hear new meanings in the rhythm and intonation of our neighbour's prayers. Simply being together week after week binds us with a thousand threads of affection, which gradually weave themselves into thick, whole cloth. Faith, hope and love pass between us like a baby; we hold them for one another in good times and bad, and somehow they are not dropped. We hold together and feel held by God.

When a friend of mine wanted to get married in a country church with which she had rather a tenuous connection, the vicar made it a condition that she and her fiancé attend at least twelve times in the months preceding the wedding. They did, and my non-churchgoing friend commented on the quality of the community she found there. 'They really know each other and care about each other!' 'Of course!' I said, amazed at her amazement.

Everyone loves a celebration. When Brenda turned 80, Andrew brought a case of champagne from France and we toasted her good health. Then Mo got an MBE, and nothing less than champagne would do for that. Christmas is all the more special because so many people join us who don't at any other time. Jubilee Brass, in their scarlet and gold, cram themselves into the old choir stalls to accompany the carols. At the end of the service, the churchyard is black and brilliant with frost and stars. Wishing 'Happy Christmas!' to a hundred people in a row, my spirits rise and rise. 'Happy Christmas to you!' say Michael and Liza. 'We won't see you now for a couple of weeks. We're going to Ephesus after Christmas, for the camel wrestling.'

— ❦ —

Epiphany

I once preached at Epiphany in the Anglican chaplaincy in Helsinki. The congregation included Finnish Lutherans and Anglicans from all over the world and, when we reached the Lord's Prayer, everyone said it in their own language (with me stretching a point and singing out in ancient Greek). It made a terrific babel of devotion. In Littlemore, most people have come from only a few streets away and many of our paths have been converging for many years, so it is harder to capture that distinctive Epiphany feeling: here we are, from different backgrounds, all arriving at the stable to be amazed.

At the start of the service, three children carefully lift the magi from where they have been waiting on the far side of the aisle and place them around the crib. A couple of lambs have to be moved out of the stable to make room. One of the children puts down his lamb, gazes at it for a moment with some concern, then gently picks the shepherd out of the stable and reunites him with his flock at the edge of the stage. Above them, a large foil star turns and winks in the draught.

I reflect that the baby Jesus is like a star, exerting a kind of gravitational force on everyone around him. People react in different ways but no one is unmoved. We shall find the same thing when he becomes an adult, and some of us feel God's presence that way, too. It pulls at the edge of our minds when we're a long way away, bothering us to take notice and change direction.

One of the things I like about the Epiphany story is that the wise men are its heroes, despite the fact that they don't fully understand what's going on and don't get everything right. I regret that we don't hear anything of their return journey. I don't believe for a moment that, having come face to face with God, they went home as T.S. Eliot suggested and waited for death in a fit of ennui with their old lives.[7] I imagine them rejuvenated, doing marvellous things in Arabia or Mesopotamia or wherever they are supposed to have come from. We have our own journey to make, of which each Christmas is just the beginning. I make a belated new year's resolution to try to keep imagining the star, as the year goes on, travelling ahead of us, pulling us ever closer to the presence of God.

Twelfth Night

The magi bring their offerings, and I
tidy my offerings away. The shepherds,
ox and ass have left the stage;
a packing case houses the flock
of Palestinian refugees.
The star stripped of its radiance is a cross,
the choir of angels in the trees
night birds in winter voice.

Please stay a little longer
before the desert and the devil call.
Glory burned out my eyes; all I can see
is rain dropping from my Christmas wreath
and, through the window, thorns.
Please stay a little longer, till my feet
find some direction in this January
dark.

      I stumble on the stony path.
The trees stretch down their roods, uplifting me.

Third Sunday of Epiphany

One of the consolations of an English January is getting up in the dark and watching dawn break. The radio chatters about farming as I stump downstairs, snap on the kitchen switch and create light. Cloistered in visibility, I pour a glass of orange juice and make a pot of tea. While I'm waiting for the tea to brew, I open the window and a chill breath of wind moves over my face. What kind of a day will it be?

The outlines of the garden emerge blackly against deep blue. The sleeping skeleton of the willow tree and, underneath, a heap of still-glowing leaves. A few puckered rosehips from the last roses, which I didn't bother to dead-head. The other berries were finished before Christmas by the birds. I find myself thinking about the last trump. I'm not sure I would want those leaves to leap back on to their branches or my breath to jump back into my body. Living, loving, labouring, we earn our rest. Heaven had better be an entirely new creation. I don't mind my atoms and energies being reused.

The moon directly overhead is whiter than a diamond, but from one corner of the sky a tide of aquamarine spills westwards, frothing with pink clouds. I step outdoors, where one or two hardy birds are singing. Seeing it born, it's hard to take the day for granted; you feel protective towards it as well as part of it. This double perspective—seeing half with the Creator's eye and half with the eye of creation—defines our humanity, wonderful and limited thing that it is. It's half past seven, and time I was on my way to the early service.

Candlemas

2 February is a day of transition. The Presentation of Christ in the Temple marks the end of the Epiphany season and the end of stories about Jesus as a child. From now on, our Gospel readings will be about Jesus the man. We keep the feast in its traditional form of Candlemas, processing and blessing the candles that we shall use in church in the coming year. I seize the chance to show off my new pink stole, which is embroidered with lilies and patches of Marian blue.

Whether in church or at home, candles come into their own in winter. The darker the world, the more brightly they shine, and the colder the air, the more powerfully we feel their heat. Another seasonal consolation is a good feast, so at Oriel College, where I work (which is properly called the College of St Mary the Virgin), we keep Candlemas with our main feast of the year. It marks the beginning of the end of winter.

The garden, too, is on the cusp. After weeks of regular frosts, the ground is softening and snowdrops and crocuses are beginning to show buds. I recall that snowdrops are sometimes called Candlemas bells, and decide that they would make a good visual aid for a sermon, but the plants in my garden are nowhere near flowering. Local flower shops yield nothing, either. It will have to be a trip to Waterperry.

The old London Road climbs Headington Hill to the north of Littlemore, then tails off in a muddy track over Shotover Edge. One stormy summer afternoon on this road, I saw the ruined colossus of a rainbow: two broken pillars and a fragmented arch strewn across the sky like a reproach to faith. Today the sky is dull white, the woods on each side damply black. As the road drops down into Wheatley, woods give way to fields. A reckless bluetit chases its mate almost under my bicycle wheel.

Waterperry garden centre has not only snowdrops in pots but acres of snowdrops in flower in its formal gardens. As I walk round, I am struck again by how perfectly adapted they are to their season. The first green spears look so fragile, but they're strong enough to push through hard ground. Snow and rain slip harmlessly off bell-shaped blooms, and slender necks remain unbroken by winter gales. Responding to the subtlest increase in light, they provide food for early insects and shelter for the more tender plants that follow them. Unlike so many people, snowdrops seem to know exactly why they're here and how they should live.

A snowdrop is not only beautiful in itself: it is a sacrament, the sign of a universe where everything is connected; every-thing has a reason and a season; everything fits together in one pattern of flower and leaf and seed, summer and winter, death and rebirth. That deep unity of things, in which every-thing is both fully itself and part of everything else, is one of the most profound discoveries we make about our world.

I get out a pen and start jotting down sermon ideas. Some people would say that the unity and harmony of the world points to a Creator God behind it all. Others would say that life itself is God—God's self-expression, God's thought and word made flesh, God's body. In the beginning, John says, was *ho logos*. We usually translate *ho logos* as 'the Word', but the Greek means far more than that. It means (among other things) creative reason, discourse, a divine command, divine wisdom, the pattern of a mind that is expressed in speech. In the beginning, says John, was wisdom; and when wisdom expressed her thoughts, they became being, and the being was the created world. So creation was full of life, and that life was a light which enlightened and guided the world towards recognising the God from whom it came. And the light shone, even in the darkness.

Snowdrops, like candles, are the light of the winter world, expressions of God that enlighten us and help us to understand God. Like any light—like anything that is doing perfectly what it is designed to do—they shine out as a beacon. The same quality, I think, is also what John saw in Christ. He was a human being who grew into everything that God intended human beings to be. He was deeply rooted in the world, taking from it what he needed and giving back what he could. He loved to see other beings flourish and rejected everything that blighted and damaged them—war, injustice, greed, indifference, hatred. He was human life as it should be, full of grace and truth, glorious with the *logos* of God. He lit up the world and showed other people the meaning of God in creation.

How much of that did Mary guess when she dedicated her firstborn in the temple? Simeon and Anna saw it and praised God. Simeon also warned Mary that a sword would pierce her soul. It is the cusp of the year, and 'cusp' means not only a threshold but also a sharp point and the horns of a dilemma. The spring will bring Mary both joy and suffering, glory and agony.

Thinking about cusps, I trip over a fallen branch, drop my pen and stumble into a patch of snowdrops. I look down in dismay at the crushed leaves, the broken stems, the bruised and torn heads. And I wonder why it seems so terrible to destroy a snowdrop, yet every day—with war and injustice and greed and indifference and hatred—we destroy ourselves and each other, and think so little of it.

— ❦ —

Gifts of the Spirit

February brings high winds, which blow strange things into my garden—a bright pink frisbee, a large square of polystyrene, a chunk of what looks like someone's shed roof. One morning, I find my washing-line pole, which I've been looking for in a desultory way for several years, lying in the middle of the garden path. I suppose I should have looked behind the drainpipe.

Fragments of other people's lives prise my imagination open like a tin. I find myself wondering who played with the frisbee, with what brother or sister, parent or friend. Who got what new piece of machinery, padded with polystyrene, for Christmas? I am worried about that shed: there's almost bound to be something in it that will spoil in the rain. Suddenly I have an enlarged sense of the world and more sympathy with my neighbours. It's an odd, random gift of the weather. I reflect that the wind of the Spirit blows where it wills and often presents us with gifts we have not asked for. We accept them for whatever message, divine or otherwise, we read in them.

I am invited to my father's at Sandford for dinner. The farmhouse kitchen glows at the end of its dark track; the table is vivid with a Provençal cloth and dishes of steaming vegetables. Prue is the only person I know who is equally good at recommending a book and choosing a silk scarf, listening to someone in deep distress and hosting a dinner party. She and our youngest sister, Anna, our father's second family, are high on Catharine's and my list of gifts of the Spirit.

Outside the church next day, the north wind thrashes the branches of the cedar and claws at my face like a cat. Clive emerges and tells me warmly that I always remind him of Joan of Arc when I celebrate.

'Really?' I say, startled. 'I don't...'

'Or perhaps,' he says thoughtfully, 'a Transylvanian missionary.'

Words fail me. It transpires that Clive has been watching old Dracula films—something about a village maiden who is going to be staked through the heart but is saved in the nick of time by a female missionary who shoots the villagers. (*Can this be right?*) But then, Clive explains, Dracula falls for the missionary. At this point, Doreen emerges to say goodbye, so I miss the end of the story.

'It's odd,' says Clive, 'that we don't talk much about Transylvania. We talk a lot about heaven and Hades, and Nirvana [*do we?*], but not Transylvania.'

'No,' I agree faintly, 'it doesn't seem to come up much, in church.'

'And yet,' says Clive, 'it's very real to some people.'

Suddenly I am listening with both ears, because he's right. There are any number of modern myths about good and evil, and many people don't see the story of Christianity as preferable to that of Dracula or Spiderman. What are we doing to address them?

Clive is another gift of the Spirit. Like Mary in her group home, and Derek who walks the Iffley Road on an unending pilgrimage towards inner peace, Clive sees the world from places most of us have never been, and reports from them with devastating candour. He has brought a bottle of water for me to bless, so that he can give it to his girlfriend, who is not well. We take it up to the altar and do it formally, incorporating prayers for them both.

When it hasn't been violently windy this week, it's been unseasonably mild. Half of me is relieved, while half worries about global warming. In the recent winds, too, homes and possessions have been destroyed and several people have died. Nothing shows us more vividly how fragile we are, how frail the web of brick and glass we weave to shelter ourselves. Was that destruction a movement of the Spirit, too? If so, the message it brought was a grim warning.

Ash Wednesday

The Book of Common Prayer instructs that the Collect for Ash Wednesday be said every day during Lent:

Almighty and everlasting God, who hatest nothing that thou hast made, and dost forgive the sins of all them that are penitent: Create and make in us new and contrite hearts, that we worthily lamenting our sins, and acknowledging our wretchedness, may obtain of thee, the God of all mercy, perfect remission and forgiveness; through Jesus Christ our Lord. Amen.

In the season of soul-searching and self-criticism, this Collect strikes a note of confidence. The world is still fundamentally good; God does not hate any part of it. And God knows that on our own it is hard, if not impossible, to change our lives, letting go of what is bad and making more space for what is good. So we are not asked to transform ourselves, but only to believe we can be transformed and ask for help.

Demonstrating goodness, and on the principle that even in Lent, Sundays are feast days, John invites the rest of the clergy team to supper: Margreet, her husband Julian, Helen-Ann and her husband Myles, and me. Julian, who is a Quaker and writes plays with profound religious resonance, keeps us from too much clerical gossip. Anyway, we prefer a debate about something difficult—the paradox of the incarnation or the problem of evil. The evening is never long enough for all we want to say. John is an accomplished cook (not to mention a trained cake decorator who can make any kind of flower out of sugar). Julian also cooks wonderfully, putting Margreet and me to shame. I like to think of myself as more of a cleaner, a view that is not shared by my colleagues, since I volunteered to hoover Margreet and Julian's sitting room and broke the video player. Tonight I confine myself to saying grace.

The routine of prayer is good for the dull, bone-chilling weeks when spring seems far away. Every day I repeat, 'Almighty and everlasting God, who hatest nothing that thou hast made…' and remind myself that whether or not I *feel* recreated today is not the only consideration. Prayers are our partners in the dance of our religious life. When we are full of faith, they help us express it, and when we stumble and break things, they support us. Hand in hand, we live and move to the elusive music of the Spirit.

Temptations

Turning out a drawer, my mother comes upon an old black-and-white postcard of Jericho. It shows the remains of an ancient settlement—a scribble of stone walls clinging to the side of a conical mountain, which is labelled 'Mount of the Temptations'. Just out of shot are Bethany and the River Jordan, where Jesus was baptised before being driven into the wilderness by the Spirit.

I preach on the temptations: how the devil tries to persuade Jesus to use his power for his private convenience, to impress the public or to gain political power. We sometimes think of these as temptations which Jesus overcomes at the beginning of his ministry and then can forget. Nothing could be further from the truth. Throughout his life, Jesus faces the same temptations again and again. Even in his last week, he is tempted to give the Jews a sign to prove he is the Messiah—to take on the Roman political authorities—to evade crucifixion. He resists.

His reasons are always the same. His power, and his work, are not his own but God's. He serves and worships nothing and no one but God, and he teaches the disciples that serving God means forgetting self-interest and self-gratification. 'If any want to become my followers, let them deny themselves and take up their cross and follow me.'[8] 'The Son of Man came not to be served but to serve, and to give his life a ransom for many.'[9]

In the vestry after the service, a brisk discussion is in progress. Who is giving up what for Lent? The ordinands are giving up variously wine, caffeine and chocolate. If I give up chocolate in the middle of term, I say, I won't get to the end. I remember fondly a sign I saw once on the road to St David's: 'Pemberton's Chocolate Farm'. At last, I thought, they've worked out how to breed chocolate. I saw happy visions of cows giving chocolate milk and hens laying chocolate eggs. The weaknesses that haunt me most are selfishness, time-wasting and lack of charity. I don't suppose I'll beat them in the next six weeks but I'm going to try to abstain as much as possible.

The tradition of giving things up for Lent has gone rather out of fashion in recent years. Better, people say, to do something positive for somebody. Serving others is, of course, central to the gospel and, at a clergy team meeting the following week, we agree to make it the theme of our Pentecost season, when we are practising following in the footsteps of the earliest Christians. Lent has another purpose. This is the time of year when we practise giving up ourselves—the temptation to use our gifts and resources for private gratification, or to impress others, or to exert power over them. Such temptations are always with us. We pray for the strength to respond as Jesus did, that the meaning and fulfilment of our lives may come not from serving ourselves, but always and only from serving God.

— ❦ —

Silence and solitude

We are keeping Lent with silence before the main Communion service. To a few people, it comes naturally. Jean observes one day that when her husband died, people expected her to have the radio or television on at all hours, but she doesn't; she keeps silence. Most people, though, find silence harder than they expect. The problem is not praying voicelessly in words, which is quite easy, but emptying our heads of words and simply being there—waiting, listening, being aware of God's presence or absence. It takes practice.

I meditate on Elijah, who went into the desert, climbed to the top of Mount Horeb and met God not in wind, earthquake or fire but in silence. The wind and storm seem to me outward signs of Elijah's inner turmoil and his busy, conflicted, complicated life. It's only when he lets it all go and settles down in solitude to listen that he can hear the voice of God again.

I love the shared silence of a Friends' meeting and the highly charged sense of communion that it creates, but mostly, I am one of those who seek silence in solitude. In an empty church, for instance. You sidle in; the door closes and the air settles back around you. The sounds of the world outside are blocked by the thick walls. You drift; you wallow; you drown in silence. Your ears ring with it. It squeezes the space around you like a shout. Then, as your ears adjust, you begin to hear the space in this silence, the size of it. You feel how small you are and how vast the silence is. It reaches out into infinity. You are listening to the movements of the stars.

A pew creaks. You realise how much there is to hear in silence. Each sound registers separately, distinctly. You are deafened, as Nina Cassian said, by dust falling on furniture, by the inching of the light across the floor.[10] The bark of a car, the purr of your breath and, behind and between them, silence, trickling in, expanding, forcing atom from atom.

You are tuning back into silence itself. It moves; it ripples. It rolls over you in waves. It rings with a music slower and more intense than any music you can hear. It beats through your body, reshaping you to its tune. It makes you want to dance. It's like the arms of God enfolding you, absorbing, sweeping you off your feet.

You realise that silence is not silence at all but the rhythm of the universe, the song that coordinates particles and binds atoms. It is the tide on which we are created, in which we live and die and are eternally remade. It is the voice that we call God and the voice of God in us, and we are the expression of the song's meaning.

Then you are back, standing in a quiet church, wondering if moments have passed, or hours.

St David's Day

Spring, as defined by the Meteorological Office, has arrived, and I take a walk up the river to look for signs. The sky is as grey and opaque as the lid on a Tupperware box, the water fudge-brown with silt, the willows tangled and dripping. The weather is keeping Lent. In Iffley churchyard, though, crocuses burn purple and gold like puffs of natural gas ignited by the March sun. The birds are singing plainsong. Easter is surely coming!

Drifts of heart-shaped confetti show that, for one happy couple, a new life has already begun. The confetti is non-biodegradable and I catch myself thinking that, buried in the crevices of the wall, it may even outlast the marriage. I try the church door but it is locked. It doesn't matter: the desert is always open. Anyone can go in and stay for as long as they like.

Leaf buds are sleeping soundly on the ancient horse chestnut by the church gate. No trumpet rouses them. It is not time. How long, Lord? Winter has almost exhausted our reserves. We wait, not daring to calculate how much longer we can last.

'Watch and pray.' Advent's motto is good for Lent, too. But I am too tired to pray; even the short step into silence seems a marathon. I am tempted to sit down under the chestnut tree and hope that the new life which touches it one sunny morning will quicken me too. Instead, I turn homewards. 'O Lord, you have searched me and known me. You know when I sit down and when I rise up; you discern my thoughts from far away...'[11] The desert behind and in front of me stretches for ever. Faith boxes and coxes with doubt. We both know and can't know that Easter will come. I keep an only half-sceptical eye out for angels.

The beginning of spring means that it is almost the end of term. My students, too, are tired, and say they are looking forward to going home. A lucky few are heading south over Easter, to explore Greece or Italy. I preach at college evensong on St David, whose horse could walk on water and who raised springs from dry ground and turned them into Communion wine—or so his eleventh-century supporters claimed, while using him to back their bid for episcopal authority over the British Church. They lost out to Canterbury, but St David was established for ever as the patron saint of Wales. The University's spring boat races, 'Torpids', took place this week, and members of the choir who are also oarsmen confide that they are a bit hoarse after their Torpids dinner last night. The men's first boat had to drown the sorrow of going down two places in the rankings, and the women's, one.

In the desert

I

The first word should be
Yes! but it is always No.
Get you behind me! I had to come. I had to go.

Never believe, because I am not with you
you are not here. Your breath
carries forever on its atomic tide; deep in the desert
words still slowly through my silence
burning the tongue.

What hollow soul
denies those whom it loves, leaves those who love it?
Who chooses emptiness and deprivation
over life?

Life! Where your pulse makes music with a passing pulsar,
particles dance glittering with the shiftless sands
and every dart of light ignites a vision

in the hollow of God's hand.

II

The first temptation
is to make friends with Satan
out of compassion. Being alone, his loneliness
older than deserts, helpless as a snake

crawling from its cold rock at dawn, wrings the warm-
                                              blooded
human heart. Besides
with nothing between you and nothing, someone to talk to
seems a harmless desire.
Age after age
Satan squats in his ashes, for such sweets
of kindly innocence to wander by.

III

What will it be, the payoff? New life?
A new vocation? That historic prize,
the call to prophecy?

High on a holy hill he prances
as he prattles, nimble as a goat,
relishing company.

It might be martyrdom, or virtuous
obscurity. It might be a delusion…
How will you know, just out of interest?

Or have we given talking up for Lent?

I did not come to make myself
a present of myself, or pick vocation
gift-wrapped off some symbolic tree.

What, then?
                  To see if you were real.

I don't need to be real: people
can do that for me. But what if
Santa Claus doesn't exist?

What will you do
if after forty days no one has spoken?

IV

For the damage I have done,
For the good I failed to do,
For what I am, have been, and might have been
I come to grieve

where night relieves self of itself
and I no longer need patrol my skin;
desire is dead in my heart's prison
and every sand-dogged step dissolves
under its own intention.

                    Come
drop your definitions where
they will not be found, and wait
where motive means no more than motion.
Waiting is the place: the inconceivable
portal of heaven.

Mothering Sunday

Mothering Sunday is a major festival at Littlemore. By a quarter to ten, the church is already full. The service begins with a parade of army cadets and Brownies, who march their flags down the aisle and present them to the vicar to be propped behind the altar. As it is Lent, the church is bare, so the flags and uniforms add a welcome splash of colour. So too do half a dozen buckets of garden flowers, which are lined up in front of the screen. At the end of the service, all the children help to give out posies, first to their own mothers and then to every woman in the church.

My mother receives her posy—two daffodils, a sprig of forsythia and a few grape hyacinths—with relish. More than anyone I know, she has a gift for celebrating the wonderful in the ordinary. Whether she is teaching students or cooking for friends, weeding the garden or making greeting cards, she makes an art of everyday living. Everyone around her benefits from her mindfulness.

We take the view, at St Mary and St Nicholas, that there are many ways to mother a parish. Today we also celebrate those who keep an eye on their parents and neighbours, visit and shop for them; those who run mother-and-toddler groups, youth groups and sports clubs; those who cook community lunches, raise money for good causes or listen to children read each week in school; those who minister in church, in schools and in hospitals. Some of them have children of their own and some do not, but all of them are devoted, hard-working and tough.

I reflect on Mary, who was also tough. Even when her grown-up son snubbed her in public—even when, for all his wisdom, he did not recognise that she was as much the Lord's servant as he—she would not let him go. In John's Gospel, it is only Mary and John who dare to stay with Jesus for all those hours as he hangs on the cross. In art, it is always Mary who receives Jesus' body as it is taken down from the cross, and, although that scene is not in the Gospels, it seems inevitable and right. In Matthew, Mark and Luke, Mary may be (in the apocryphal Gospel of Philip, she is) one of the women who come at dawn on Easter Sunday to embalm the body, and find the tomb empty. Perhaps, of all of them, Mary was the least surprised to find that Jesus had disappeared again on a new journey.

As a mother, Mary gives without knowing what will happen to her gift and without counting the cost. And what is true of Mary, and of her son, is also true of God. We have inherited the habit of talking about God as Father but surely, I suggest in my sermon, we should also talk about God as Mother. Some visionaries already have; Julian of Norwich even talked of Jesus as mother: 'As we know, our own mothers bore us unto pain and dying. But our true mother Jesus, who is all love, bears us unto joy and endless living ... A mother feeds her child with her milk, but our beloved mother, Jesus, feeds us with himself.' [12]

God loves as mothers love—extravagantly, pouring love out without measure. God loves intimately, each one of us as a different person, and equally, every one of us as much as all the others, however many there are. God loves completely and unreservedly, no matter what we do. In the house of God our Mother there will always be a welcome, a meal and a place to stay—and quite possibly a ticking-off and some good hard advice.

'What does Mothering Sunday mean to you?' I ask Win and Brenda after the service. Win has four grandchildren and five great-grandchildren. 'I like it,' she says. 'It's always lovely to see the children.'

After church, Catharine and I take our mother to Woodstock for lunch. The hotel is full of other mothers being taken out by their families. Fathers encourage small children to hand over pot plants. Young adults are a little self-conscious at finding themselves back in the parental nest. The middle-aged handle their elderly parents competently. The elderly accept the offered arm and the comfortable chair with appreciation, irritation or tactful tolerance, according to temperament.

After lunch, we and the other families amble round Blenheim Park. It is a brisk and breezy afternoon. Early lambs gambol about their dams. In the local art gallery, I make a bid for a decorated ostrich egg which is being auctioned for charity, and realise that Easter will be upon us before we know it.

Doorkeeping

At this time of year, a steady trickle of strangers begins to appear at Sunday services. These are not usually new regular worshippers. They are the first of the summer's wedding couples-to-be, who have come to hear their banns read. Most have little prior connection with the church, though some have been baptised here or visited on a school trip. Some are visibly nervous at finding themselves part of a service, and responses and hymn tunes are unfamiliar to them. Few will be seen again, unless to have a baby baptised and perhaps, eventually, to be buried.

To these couples, nobody is more important than the person at the door. He or she makes the difference between someone's feeling welcome and knowing what to do, and feeling bewildered or unwelcome or even assaulted. Nor is it only visitors who feel it. At the moment we enter a church, even if we go every week or every day, we are all a little vulnerable. We are full of happiness and want to share it, or depressed and want to hide; we are hopeful or grieving or searching. The special vocation of doorkeepers is to share the moment of transition from the outside world to holy space; to help us on our way to doing or saying or hearing what we need to do or say or hear that day.

'I am the door,' says Jesus in John's Gospel. 'If anyone enters by me, he will be saved.' [13] We'd like to keep the church open all the time but we are afraid of vandals, so the west door is opened daily and a prie-dieu stands in the porch with prayers on it, from which one can see into the church through a grille. Some of the prayer cards have illustrations by the artist

Elo Allik (Mrs Schünemann in private life), which make the church buildings seem to dance. 'Come in,' they say; 'rest in my rocking arms; be recreated.'

Our doorkeepers (properly known as sidespersons) are kind and practical people, and the service begins better for their attentions. Afterwards it is everyone's job to notice and welcome strangers over a cup of coffee. Standing by the chancel step, cup in hand, in a quiet moment, I look round at the knots of people chatting to each other, and I am struck by how relaxed they are. It occurs to me that we feel safe here. In this building, whether you're mad or sad, happy or anxious, well-loved or lonely, you are accepted and drawn into conversation. Few other places make us feel so welcome, so seen for who we are.

Palm Sunday

Littlemore has three churches: the Baptist chapel (which has been here longest), the Church of the Blessed Dominic Barberi (who received Newman into the Catholic Church), and St Mary and St Nicholas. We often collaborate, and once a year our ecumenism goes public with a shared Palm Sunday procession around the village.

We meet on the little green outside the chip shop. With our embroidered banners, scarlet vestments and glittering processional crosses, we are an eye-catching crowd, but the star of the show is a donkey, who arrives in a loosebox from the nearby donkey sanctuary. The children rush to help get him out. This year's donkey appears to be shy, or perhaps just cross, and it takes some time to extract him. Eventually we entice him with carrots to the head of the procession and strike out, singing, down the road towards the post office and the mini-mart. Our voices ring hollow as we pass under the ringroad. The dual carriageway stalks over us on long insect-legs. Past the Blue Mile pub and the Catholic church, still singing and waving branches of laurel in lieu of palms, we turn into the Minchery Farm estate. All along our circuitous route, children and a few adults come out to stare. Nobody laughs at us or jeers but no one smiles either. At the top of St Nicholas Road, we exchange the peace and part.

Not being one of nature's street-corner evangelists, I have mixed feelings about these occasions. They lack something of the gusto and sense of tradition of such processions in Italy or Spain. Our singing, unsupported by instruments, tends to be ragged, and the back of the column lags increasingly behind the front. As we part company, the divisions that underlie our collaboration are sadly obvious. On the other hand, there must be a hundred people in the procession, which makes not a negligible witness, and over the years we have got to know and become friends with members of each other's congregations whom we might not otherwise have met.

When we part, the Anglicans get the donkey. I have foreseen trouble getting this year's performer into church but, with a good deal of pulling and palming of more carrots, he consents to walk up the aisle. As I begin the prayer of preparation, I notice how close I am standing to his hindquarters. I keep a wary eye on his tail, and when it begins to twitch I move unobtrusively backwards. The worst happens, twice. 'I was down on my knees last week, *scrubbing* that carpet,' mourns Di after the service.

We perform a dramatic reading of the passion narrative, individuals and groups taking different roles. ('Whoever gave our hardworking Parish Church Council the role of by-standers?' I wonder.) Through the reading, slightly rough because unrehearsed, the power of the story grows until, by the end, everyone is gripped. Shaken, I haul my mind back to the service, forget one of the hymns and give the wrong acclamation during the eucharistic prayer. It's a long service and the organist, who has a rehearsal to go to, leaves before the final hymn. 'A very good service,' says everyone afterwards. Technically, I think crossly to myself, it was terrible... but the congregation have higher priorities. Sue has stripped down the Christmas tree to make a cross for the churchyard.

The churches and schools of the area get together to produce a set of stations of the cross, which are on display in the Cowley shopping centre. We meet there for an ecumenical service at 7pm. Shopping centres are uncanny places after closing time, a portent of what the city might be like after a terrorist attack or a radiation leak. Our panel, sculpted out of polystyrene by the youth club under Andrew's direction, is a relief of the head of Jesus in the tomb, swathed in metres of cheesecloth. Friends are there from this morning's procession, from Iffley and Cowley. I share a hymn book with a group of people I don't know, and wonder whether among them is a future friend. Admiring all the other churches' panels, I try to suppress a patriotic feeling that ours is the best.

Holy Week

I spend the first part of Holy Week with my aunt and uncle on their Leicestershire farm. Two cross-country trains and a bus get me there in time for lunch; the house is immaculate, my uncle is on his way in from ploughing and there are sausages in my aunt's oven. In good times and bad (and now is very bad for small farmers), their orderly lives are a work of art and a model of steadfastness. Suffering, in Paul's phrase, has produced endurance in them, and endurance, character. I am less sure, as they get older, that character has produced hope.[14]

My aunt has been given a Women's Institute wild flower survey to complete for their land—a daunting project—so I spend two days walking the fields, describing what's flowering in a representative sample of hedgerows. Among the ubiquitous celandines and field pansies are a few patches of lady's smock, just coming into bud. Violets—purple, white, and silver with purple veins—sprawl under every hedge. My tramping startles several larks that are nesting in fields of set-aside. Here and there, where in the past stood cottages with cottage gardens, cultivated daffodils and grape hyacinths are springing up in the middle of fields. They won't survive long once the cattle are let out. The Roman road is a good place to hear cuckoos: I keep one ear open but am not lucky this year.

My cousins have been to the funeral in a nearby village of a twelve-year-old who used to play rugby with cousin Tim. Five hundred people packed the church. Farming relationships go back for generations; most of my aunt's and uncle's closest friends are children they played with or boys and girls they dated. Their society has a complexity and depth that most of us can hardly imagine nowadays.

After supper, I wander down the village in the last of the daylight and see lights on in the church, so I try the door and walk in on a Holy Week service. Of course! Having made rather a lot of noise coming in, I feel it's only civil to stay. The vicar reads from a modern retelling of the Passion, which pretends to take the 'common-sense' viewpoint: Jesus was a troublemaker who had to be stopped, and so on. At the end, I consider whether to slip out or stop and say hello. I resolve to be sociable, and introduce myself. The vicar rattles off a list of Holy Week services and urges me to come again. She doesn't know my cousins, because they don't go to church and she confines her parish to those who do. They know this and resent it—another place where village life is wearing thin. 'Who is my neighbour in the modern village?' I wonder as I stroll back up the dark hill.

Maundy Thursday

Maundy Thursday is a glorious day, brilliant after frost, warm as summer by the afternoon. I dash about town in my shirt-sleeves, buying Easter eggs and photocopying the Easter Eve service. We meet at 7pm in the still-balmy vicarage garden. Julian has made leek and potato soup for 25 people and we break bread together. Brother mosquito and sister midge do their best to eat us alive.

After the meal we walk over to church for the Eucharist. Then we strip the altar till it looks like a tomb, and settle down to keep a silent vigil till midnight. Sue, Hilary and Ivy have made a monstrance six feet high out of trestles and wrought-iron candelabra, crammed with dozens of lilies and laurel branches, studded with scores of candles. In the middle, the sacrament is entombed in its wooden box. It must have taken half the day to build. When the lights go down, it glows like an angelic presence.

Other people's silence always looks more tranquil than one's own. Stretching my legs to ease my back, I am aware of Wendy's absorbed stillness across the aisle. A draught from the west door fingers my ankles and creeps up my trouser legs. Greta and Ray seem not to notice it. People come and go. Sianne, who at six years old has a taste for grown-up liturgy, is exhausted but doesn't want to leave; she insists on staying for an hour, gazing raptly at the glimmering flowers, before Marie takes her home. Judith and Martin return in the middle of the evening. Quietness radiates from them. We used to have a curate who had to leave every so often for a cigarette. Rumour had it, he went for a pint just before closing time to get him through the last hour.

I reflect on the kind of prayers appropriate to this watch. Silent prayer is often about feeling the presence of Christ or waiting for him. 'Maranatha. Come, Lord.' But tonight, in imagination, we are already with Jesus. Our prayers are more to do with fortifying ourselves for the disaster that we know will fall, somehow, sometime, soon.

I play with images for self-fortification. 'Wall-building prayer' sounds too rigid, as if one might end up walled in. 'Self-arming prayer' sounds too aggressive (though I remind myself that Paul's armour of light is mostly defensive). 'Muscle-building prayer' captures the meaning of what we're doing—making ourselves strong to deal with the future—but is dreadfully pedestrian.

The third hour approaches and it becomes dangerous to close my eyes. The sound of the gas heaters is like someone running a hot bath in the next room... I struggle on and, a quarter of an hour later, am wide awake again.

Perhaps the aim of our prayers tonight is balance—like in those martial arts where you can't be defeated because you can never be knocked over by your opponent. We're doing spiritual T'ai Chi, I tell myself whimsically. Our sense of God grounds us and keeps returning us to the upright. The thought lifts my heart and, for a while, praying is easy. I know it won't last long so I enjoy it while it does. Good moods and bad, high and low, are just phases we go through.

As the last hour slips away, I feel the slight sadness that I expect I shall feel as I approach death. I wish I'd prayed better, had more faith. Our watch is drawing to an end. At midnight we blow out the candles, lock the doors and depart into the darkness without speaking.

— ❧ —

Good Friday

This darkest day of the year is often gloriously sunny. The weather jinx on British bank holidays doesn't seem to afflict the Easter weekend. As we arrive for the two o'clock service, the churchyard is full of children eating hot cross buns. At their one o'clock service they have made coloured paper footprints, each with their own name on, which now lead from the nave to what will be the Easter garden. We therefore walk, literally and appropriately, in their footsteps as we venerate the cross, taking it in turns to lay flowers and light candles.

Everyone has their own way of venerating the cross, just as everyone has their own way of receiving Communion. Some of us kneel before it as if asking for its blessing. Some kiss the wood in love and submission: 'May I, too, do your will.' Some lay a hand on the upright in an intimate gesture of grief, as if to comfort Christ, or perhaps Mary, or the innocent tree itself.

I preach about all the times when God has been tempted to give up on humankind, and has not. From generation to generation in the Bible, God cared for human beings, who made such a mess of their lives and were capable of such great grief and repentance. They listened to what God said and went their own way—until, by grace, a man came into the world whose faithfulness transformed it. Here was a man who would not let go of God, whatever happened; who forced good out of the deepest suffering by refusing to give up his love of God and his trust in God's goodness. Here was a man who, seemingly destroyed by evil, held fast to the people he loved, refusing to believe that evil could overcome them. No wonder God loved him: this was the Son he had always hoped for.

No one is unaffected by unconditional love. If someone has loved us completely and unshakeably, we must be changed. We live the rest of our lives knowing that we can be, have been, wholly lovable. Love buries itself in our hearts; it works on us; it makes it impossible for us not to believe in love—and, believing in it, we will always, eventually, express it in our lives. On the cross, Christ made it impossible for us to reject God's love for ever. We can only choose how long we hold out against it. No wonder his last word, according to John, was, 'It is finished.' 'It is accomplished.'[15] A word of resignation perhaps; of relief; but also of satisfaction, even triumph. A sound of trumpets on the other side.

Great and Holy Saturday

Western churches don't have much to say about Holy Saturday. There is no official Catholic or Anglican liturgy for this day; there is some theological writing about it but very little compared with what is written about Good Friday or Easter Sunday. It can become a day of garish secularism in the midst of deep mourning—when, not having to be in church, we go out and buy Easter eggs. In Orthodox churches, however, Great and Holy Saturday is given its full weight. This year in Littlemore, we keep the day with a liturgy of our own.

A dozen people meet in the cold, stripped, half-lit chancel. We descend in imagination to hell, where some traditions say that Jesus spent Saturday freeing the souls of those who had already died.

Out of the depths I cry to you, O Lord.
Lord, hear my voice!
Let your ears be attentive
to the voice of my supplications!

I wait for the Lord, my soul waits,
and in his word I hope;
my soul waits for the Lord
more than those who watch for the morning.[16]

Together we say:

Today we stand with the dead
who turned away from God.

We rejected God's gifts.
We disobeyed God's laws.
We chose our own way
and it led to hell.

I am Adam. I am Eve. I am Cain. I am David. I am Sodom. I am
Jerusalem.
We preferred our way to God's and it led us to hell.

Judy reads from Lamentations and Julian from Psalm 139,
interspersed with our own words of grief and hope. Some of
them are borrowed from Orthodox liturgies:

Hell cries out, groaning,
I should not have accepted the son of Mary!
He comes to destroy my power.
He shatters the gates of brass;
he stretches his hand out to souls that I held captive.
He lifts them up!

Hell cries out, groaning,
My power is broken!
I swallowed the living God like one of the dead,
but I cannot hold him.

Leaving the chancel, we return to earth, and stand around the
sealed tomb. We listen to Matthew's account of Saturday, the
sealing of the stone and setting of the guard. Now we stand
with the living who put the Son of God to death. Another
day dawns; the sun rises, but God is no longer with us. We
follow our routines but no one watches us, searches for us or
recognises us.

Who are we, if we no longer have a father?
Where are we, if we are no longer seen?
Adrift among the barren planets and the dying stars.

So much of what we did
we did because of God, or despite God, or to spite God.
Now we have executed Emmanuel,
it does not matter
what we do. There are no bounds to test,
no truths to doubt.
God is no longer with us.
Jesus is dead. What now?

The biggest step for humankind
is not from hope to glory,
but from nothing to hope,
and that is one
we cannot take alone.
But hope is in his grave. What now?

We ask for mercy with sudden fervour. Then we settle down again to wait.

Easter Eve

Easter Eve. An epic evening service, starting in darkness. We hear the story of the exodus, Isaiah's summons to hope and Ezekiel's fierce vision of resurrection. Bishop Henry, resplendent in mitre and a bright green cope with a map of Derbyshire all over the back, retires outside to light the Easter fire, which flares dangerously in a brisk wind. Simon sings the *Exultet* to the dancing light of his son Jacob's torch.[17] They're a musical family: later, Simon's wife Rachel will sing a Bach aria for us. But first, from one tiny candle to another, we pass the Easter flame along and across the pews till the whole church is ablaze with light. Faces shine with reflected fire. The bishop performs a baptism and several confirmations before we celebrate the first Eucharist of Easter.

Grand occasion as it is, there's always something slightly odd about celebrating Easter on Saturday night. According to the Gospels, it was Sunday morning before anyone came to the tomb and found it empty. Isn't it premature to celebrate now? Or could the resurrection have happened the night before? According to prophecy, Jesus would spend three days in the tomb, which means Friday, Saturday and Sunday. But in the Jewish calendar, a day begins when darkness falls the night before, so any time on Saturday night would count as part of Sunday.

One helpful thing about tonight is that it points to the gap between the time when Jesus left the tomb and the time the empty tomb was discovered. With it go two sides of the story, the triumph and the mystery. The way Jesus leaves the tomb is wholly mysterious. After the upheavals surrounding the crucifixion, we might have expected an earthquake, or an eclipse, at least. Instead, at some point, the stone sealing the grave is quietly rolled away and Jesus walks out through the middle of the guard. It's almost playful: as if he were saying, did you think you could catch the Spirit in a shroud? Did you think you could shut God in a cave?

If the mystery of the incarnation is that the Spirit of God becomes a human body, the mystery of the resurrection is that a human body becomes the Spirit of God. It reminds us, in the middle of our grandest ritual of the year, that we can't capture God in anything made by human beings—not caves, and not doctrine or liturgy or institutions, either. But it isn't the fact that it's an institution that endears me to the church. It's a meeting place for people who are on a common journey. Juggling a cup of hot water and a sandwich after the service, I reflect that if we can't catch the Spirit in an institution, we can rely on it for company on our pilgrimage—and for our daily bread, with (on special occasions) a dab of cheese and pickle or egg mayonnaise in it.

— ❦ —

Resurrection

I was looking for
a chasm in creation: light streaming
out of inchoate chaos; an old order breaking.

It came as healing.
Lamp posts and skin and trees remembered
they were one flesh. Glowing, the brimstone
strode from its blossom bed pink as a kiss
to stir up hurricanes.
Death could not shake the tulips where they steadied
goblets of bloody light, nor break the crust
of cloud that melted on the warm horizon.
And from his tomb, the still unborn said,
'Mary, I am the way, you are the truth, we are the life;
death comes to nothing.'

Going back to Galilee (Matthew 28)

Two roads head north out of Jerusalem: the western road through Samaria and the more familiar route through Jericho, which runs alongside the River Jordan. I imagine the disciples taking the river road, turning off briefly perhaps at Bethany to tell Martha, Mary and Lazarus what has happened. They press on past Jericho, keeping together on the lonely stretches, where Jesus set the story of the good Samaritan. Past the place where, what seems a lifetime ago, John the Baptist preached and baptised people in the river. The reeds will have grown back over it by now. Past towns with names famous in Israelite history—Succoth, Shechem, Jabesh-Gilead.

Why did they go, and why then? After Good Friday, one could have understood it. Their hopes were crushed; they were terrified that they would be arrested next. After Easter Sunday, there is surely every reason to stay in Jerusalem. What might not happen now? If the risen Christ stood on the pinnacle of the temple and revealed himself to the people—if he hammered on the door of the praetorium and summoned Pilate out to meet his God—who could stop him? Who wouldn't fall down and worship him? But Christ has refused that kind of power once and he has no use for it now. He has something else in mind for the disciples. 'Go back to Galilee,' he says. 'Go home.'

They will have arrived in the northern farmlands just as the fields were turning green with spring wheat. On the lower slopes of the hills, the terraced vines are coming into flower and, higher up, they can hear the bleating of lambs.

The scent of apple and pomegranate orchards serenades the honeybees. The first place they reach is Nain, and here, perhaps, they bump into a young man loading up his donkey for market—a young man with a widowed mother.

The next village is Nazareth, and there Mary leaves them and goes home to her other children. The disciples don't linger: Jesus was nearly killed here when he preached in the synagogue. They walk on to Cana, where maybe they get a meal and a bed for the night from a couple whose wedding they attended—all except for Bartholomew, who goes home. But now everywhere is home for someone— Thaddeus, Thomas, Philip, Simon, sons of the hilltop villages with their rough roads bordered by dwarf oaks, and sparrows making their nests among the vines. They pass a man up a ladder, mending the roof of his house, who used to be a leper. In the field beyond, a man is hoeing vegetables who, this time last year, could not even walk. So many ordinary people are living lives touched and transfigured by the kingdom of God.

Eventually, the few remaining disciples will have reached the Sea of Galilee and walked along the shore, between the restless water and the quiet mountains. Perhaps they sat down in one of those natural amphitheatres where Jesus used to preach, and shared a loaf of bread. Smelt lilies somewhere nearby. Remembered Jesus stilling a storm; walking on the waves; telling them, when they were exhausted and miserable after a useless night's fishing, to put out their nets again.

They come to Capernaum, which seems almost uncannily unchanged. The market is busy, the tax collector at his table. Matthew walks quietly past and is not recognised. Zebedee sits on the seafront, mending his nets. He looks up and there are his sons. The local centurion nurses a cup of wine outside the tavern. A young girl runs down the street in front of him. Her father Jairus, still leader of the synagogue, is indoors, debating the law with a couple of men who once were possessed by demons.

Finally, Peter finds himself alone outside his own house. Maybe his mother-in-law is inside, making bread; his wife spinning, the children playing on the roof. But he hardly sees their faces or hears their shouts of astonishment and joy. Suddenly, vividly, he remembers the day he left, with Jesus.

And here and now, at last, for Peter, the resurrection truly begins. In Galilee, where Jews and Gentiles meet and the blind and lame are healed; where ordinary people have heard the voice of God and seen the heavens open and the Son of Man walking among them in clouds of glory. He hears Jesus again, saying the things he used to say: 'The kingdom of heaven has come near... Follow me, and I will make you fish for people... I send you out, to proclaim the good news... cure the sick, raise the dead, cleanse the lepers, cast out demons. You received without payment; give without payment... It is enough for the disciple to be like the teacher.'[18]

For Peter, finally, it is enough.

— ❦ —

Resurrection stories

The third Sunday of Easter takes me to Kennington to deputise for their vicar, who has gone to Cardiff to watch Wales play rugby. After the 8 o'clock service at Littlemore, I cycle round to Sandford Lock, over the river and up the lane in an unpoetic April drizzle. The lane is badly potholed and someone has circled all the holes in white, like a modern art installation. On the verges, daffodils are giving way to buttercups and cow parsley. I spot the first swallows of the spring, chasing each other over the backs of cattle grazing by the river.

Barely half a mile apart and loosely linked by a ribbon of houses and care homes, Sandford and Littlemore are about as different as two villages can be. Where we have the ringroad, Sandford has the river. Where we have estates, Sandford has water meadows. We sprawl sociably, mingling at the edges with Rose Hill and Blackbird Leys; Sandford is self-contained, a clutch of stone houses, brick villas and bungalows clustered about a tiny Norman church and surrounded by farmland.

To do justice to these differences, I reflect, we ought to foster some bitter inter-village feud. In fact, we get on extremely well, people in each village having family and friends in the other and sharing institutions like the Women's Institute and the book club.

Kennington, over the river, is different again: a comet-shaped village with a compact ancient head and a long modern tail, which streams along a narrow ledge between the water meadows and Bagley Wood. It is known locally as a strong community, with its own primary school, shops and library. In the 1950s, its medieval church was deemed too small for the expanding population, so it was turned into the church hall and a modern Italianate brick church was built beside it.

When I arrive, the church is already busy. Roger welcomes the congregation while Isabel gathers notices; Gerry is checking the readings, Sally marshalling the choir. The church is cruciform, with the altar in the middle. Regulars peer around corners into neighbouring arms to see who's here. Over the central space glowers one of the highest pulpits I have ever seen; it is never used.

There are greetings with old friends. Absence seasons our irregular meetings. I discover that the interest of a local publisher in my writing is Julia's doing, and wonder at the energy that can sustain a busy career, a family and all kinds of work for the parish. Kennington is a stronghold of the doctrine of the priesthood of all believers. Members of the congregation give hours of their time every week to look after their neighbours, the church and many other village institutions.

I preach on resurrection appearances, a daunting subject for sermons in times half-scientific and half-superstitious. What they are not about, I suggest, despite doubting Thomas, is proof—physical proof not being the currency of grace. They are stories, which in themselves are strange, elusive, powerful entities.

Stories express the meanings of our experience. Despite everything, Jesus had not deserted the disciples: he was still with them and the Spirit was on its way. Stories may have the same meanings for generations, if we go on speaking their language and sharing their experience. We walk with the Spirit still; Christ watches over us, from somewhere to which we hope our journey will take every one of us at last. They also grow meanings that those who told them first could not have bargained for, and sometimes they cease to make sense at all. Reading the book of Revelation, I sometimes feel my lips grow cold. I do not speak this language; I don't know whether I ever shall.

We go on telling stories, even if we do not understand them, because they are beautiful. Because people we have loved and trusted, trusted them with their lives. Because experience may yet come to us—a bush may burst into flame, we may hear a voice calling from heaven—and then we'll say, 'Ah, that's what those stories were talking about.' We tell them because, if they never make sense to us, our children's children may yet recover what they were meant to say.

Religious stories, I suggest, are also the ancestors of statements of faith. When we say, 'I believe in God who made heaven and earth' or, 'I believe in Jesus Christ who was raised from the dead', we are not simply making propositional statements: 'Such-and-such is the fact.' We are also saying, 'I put my trust in this story which I heard, which tells how the world is in ways no proposition could encapsulate.' We trust in stories, hope in stories, love in stories. They are the way we converse with the cosmos.

After the service, Dennis wants to know when I'll be coming to the local deaf centre. I have rashly expressed an ambition to learn to sign. What I need, I say, is two parallel lives, then I could surely fit everything in. It's outrageous how little I seem to get done in this one—and the more I dash about, the less I live. Dennis is formidably busy himself— one week playing the organ at the prison, another anchoring Kennington choir—but he has the gravity of a man who has stopped and stared a lot and sees deeply into things. He is, in his 80s, alive right the way through. I sometimes meet him wheeling his bicycle through Sandford. He grieves every day for his wife, dead some years now, and does not pretend otherwise.

Cycling home, I reflect on the fact that I have no idea what it's like to be 80 or to lose a spouse. Every day in this cluster of riverside parishes, friends tell me stories that I do not yet understand. One day, perhaps, experience will come to me, and then I'll say, 'Ah, that's what Dennis, or Phyllis, or Anna was talking about.' Meanwhile, listening to the elders enriches my view of life in ways that no effort of my own can match.

The nesting season

A blackbird is sitting on her nest in the winter honeysuckle, right outside my study window. If I dodge about a bit, peering through the leaves, I can just see her from where I sit, hatching a sermon at my desk. She looks back with a bright eye and we are very companionable. From time to time, the male arrives with food and immediately leaves again, gliding low over the garden. I wonder whether he is surprised by the fact that, among the bluebells and alliums, a few pink roses are already in flower.

I have a new next-door neighbour. This is her first house and she too is nesting: I hear her bustling about at weekends, arranging furniture and hammering picture hooks into the walls. We too are companionable, catching sight of each other through the hedge as we make morning tea or chop vegetables for supper. Later in the summer, we are going to tackle the hedge from her side, where it has been allowed to grow wild. Dramatic spikes of an unknown but very thorny shrub have shot up, loaded with creamy flowers, to spear the sky.

I imagine the Sermon on the Mount taking place in spring, with Jesus pointing to the busily foraging birds and the tranquil lilies of the field. After the silence and stillness of Lent and Holy Week, this is a busy time of year. We are planning fêtes and outings, booking holidays, planting out seedlings, literally or metaphorically sowing all the things we hope to reap later in summer. Reading Luke, I come across the story of Mary and her sister Martha, who told Jesus off for letting Mary sit and listen to him when there was work to be done. 'Let her sit,' Jesus said. You don't always have to be up and doing. Look at the lilies of the field. At this time of year, it is worth being reminded not always to be busy, but sometimes just to be together with our friends and neighbours, listening and being companionable.

The Latin Communion

It is my turn to take the termly Latin Communion at the University Church. This service (an ordinary Prayer Book Communion in everything but language) exists because, at the Reformation, Oxford argued that Latin was in everyday use here and that a service in Latin was therefore in the vernacular. Services in Latin continue to this day, though it cannot be said to have been anyone's vernacular for some time.

I robe in the vestry under the disapproving eyes of Victorian vicars and the friendlier ones of the steward and pro-vice-chancellor. The steward informs me that he will not take Communion because, as a Protestant, he feels it improper to take the sacraments when he has not understood the service. I nod acceptance and stifle an impulse to shake his hand. I too suffer from doubts about this service, even while the part of me that loves Latin delights in using it.

About 30 people line the slightly draughty chancel (the roof has recently started to let heat out and water in). Some of those present will be tourists, some ordinands, some students. I wonder why they are here. To catch some flavour of the Reformation? To take part in an Oxford tradition? Perhaps, like me, they come to connect, however loosely, a dead language and culture, which they admire and study, with their living faith.

After the service I take off my dog collar and cross the road to begin the day's teaching. Down narrow Oriel Street, where the houses are all different and all painted in spring colours, and into Oriel Square. I salute the plaque that commemorates Bill Turpin: Rhodes scholar, diplomat, railroad builder, benefactor, and delightful and much-missed friend. The ghosts of apple trees whisper from Christ Church's Peckwater Quad, which used to be Oriel's garden and orchard.

When I was first ordained, I assumed that my experience as a university lecturer would inform the way I preached and taught in the parish, while my pastoral training for ordination might change the way I related to my students. In the event, the opposite happened. I found that I couldn't preach as I lectured—experimentally, playfully, acting as devil's advocate to challenge my students. I could only try to be clear and very honest. It made me think hard about what I taught and why. On the other hand, I found that, as a priest, it was all too easy to fall into a kind of pastoral roleplay, in which I was always smiling and comfortable words came less from the heart than from the dog collar. But when my students had problems, they came to me because they wanted my honest opinion, the benefit of my lived experience, however limited. Gradually I found myself trying to listen to my parishioners more as I would listen to my students—without pretending to be wiser than I was.

There are expected and unexpected consequences of being a 'minister in secular employment'. Many MSEs hope that they will become a spiritual or pastoral resource for people at work, and many do, but you can't predict who will be interested in your ministry, who indifferent and who offended by it. The most unexpected people, when you are thinking about the job and not about God or religion at all, turn to you as a priest.

I once took the train with a colleague to a meeting in London. We were deep in discussion of our current research when my colleague said, 'It struck me last night that when I die, I'd like you to take my funeral.' Nothing had been further from my mind. 'Really...? Of course—I'd love to,'

I stammered. 'I mean, I wouldn't love to, obviously... be very sad... hope it won't happen for years... Splendid... I mean, not splendid...' I don't remember how I extricated myself but the memory still makes me squirm. Once you're ordained, you forget it, even for a moment, at your peril.

That raises questions. Is your secular job compatible with being a priest? If so, how should it be done? What are you saying, by the way you speak and act, about the relationship between God and faith and the world?

But these are not questions for MSEs only. Like the language of the Eucharist, they belong equally to all Christians. So I put together a parish course to help us think more about the way we live and witness in our everyday lives. We call it 'Apostello', meaning 'I send you out' (after Matthew 10:16), and it runs jointly with Sandford in the early summer. The group meets weekly in the church, which is, mercifully, just warm enough by May to be pleasant.

We talk about the role of prophecy in contemporary society, whether we are called to act as prophets in the places where we live and work, and, if so, how best to do it. Many Christians are natural pastors and spend a lot of time listening to friends and colleagues. We reflect on what makes a good listener—when and when not to advise—and on how to recognise when people need more support than we can give.

Everything we do depends on our own practice of faith, and especially on prayer. We spend two weeks discussing how we pray. I enthuse about the practice of 'praying without ceasing'. Everyone can practise entwining prayer with action until, one day, the two become indistinguishable and all our actions are simply expressions of our love of God.

None of the group favours aggressive evangelism—telling people what to believe, or that they will go to hell if they don't believe it—but we practise articulating our own faith in readiness for the times when we are asked about it. It's surprisingly difficult. Could we, for instance, sum up our faith in a sentence or two, for someone who knows nothing about it? Is there perhaps a verse from the Bible that captures something of the essence of what we believe? The only person who can come up with one instantly is Ray: 'Ask, and it will be given to you; search, and you will find; knock, and the door will be opened for you.'[19] The rest of us nod appreciatively but have to go away for a week to think of our own verse. The course is felt to be useful, and there is talk of other parishes doing it next year.

Local saints

I seize an unforecast day of sunshine by taking a walk down the river to visit some of our local saints. Oxfordshire is not famous for its saints, perhaps because we are an inland people. We do not, like the Celts, watch the sun setting over western seas and burn to throw ourselves into the arms of God. Nor, like the people of the east coast, were we martyred in scores during Viking invasions. But we have a handful of saints of our own, and the best-known are linked by the River Thames.

Furthest to the west lies Beornwald, a martyr of the eighth century who is enshrined at Bampton, where Oxford's patron saint Frideswide once kept pigs. Downstream, we come to Binsey, and Frideswide's holy well. A mile or so further on, the river passes through the centre of Oxford, by Frideswide's shrine in the cathedral.

I pick up the pilgrim route on the south side of town. The sloping fields beyond Sandford Lock are yellow with rape and blue-green with wheat. A fringe of last summer's stubble stands round the edges, stiff as peroxide hair, brown at the roots. Nuneham Courtney, on the hilltop, has been suffering from floods, which have never affected it before; they are blamed on global warming.

Abingdon is home to several saints. Ethelwold, Elstan and Alric were monks of the abbey here in the tenth century, while Edmund was born here in 1170. He taught at Oxford (where St Edmund's College bears his name) and eventually became Archbishop of Canterbury. Shocked by the corruption he found in church and state, he protested to the king and the papal legate. When they told him to get real, or 13th-century words to that effect, he left the country in protest and died in Burgundy. I ponder the pros and cons of gesture politics as I amble between moored pleasure boats and children eating ice creams. Edmund is said to have seen visions and, on his deathbed, to have declared to God, 'I have sought nothing else but you.'

At Abingdon, the afternoon warms up. The riverbank smells of recent mowing and the water winks at the sun. I appreciate the change more for having been walking for several hours, and having watched the dew dry and the colours deepen and the sun soar slowly across the sky. Nothing creates value like time. And the good things that come with time cannot be hurried or artificially produced; they have to be got to by living. One of the great acts of faith in our lives—of trust and hope—is being prepared to take time, to wait for good things to emerge from long experience.

A turn of the river after Abingdon brings the towers of Didcot power station into view, steaming like cauldrons and dwarfing Culham's unpretentious church. I am getting a blister and my rucksack is hanging annoyingly off one shoulder. The tufted tops of the Wittenham Clumps, rising abruptly out of the plain, are a welcome sign that I am approaching Dorchester.

Birinus was a Roman bishop who came to England in 634. He had planned a mission to the Midlands, but the people of Wessex kept him so busy that he never got there. A local king called Cynegils, whom he baptised, gave him Dorchester-on-Thames as his episcopal see. It was an important town then; now it is a pretty village with wet feet and an abbey church well-known for concerts and art exhibitions. On my way to pay my respects to the saint, I pass, in a side aisle, an inscription commemorating one Sarah Fletcher, who died in 1799 in her 29th year. 'Reader!' commands the stone. 'If thou haft a Heart fam'd for Tenderness and Pity, contemplate this spot…' Sarah was apparently a paragon of beauty and gentleness, 'but when Nerves were too delicately fpun to bear the rude Shakes and Jostlings which we meet with in this Transitory World, Nature gave way. She funk and died, a Martyr to Exceffive Senfibility.' I register a twinge of sympathy for Mrs Fletcher's family.

According to his biographer, Birinus 'was a good and just man, who in carrying out his duties was guided more by an inborn love of virtue than by what he read in books'. Dorchester has been lucky in its bishops. One of Birinus' successors was Elwin, whose sister and three brothers were also saints.

A friend of mine went to Dorchester Abbey to hear her marriage banns read and came out saying, 'They kept *on* talking about St Birinus. As if he was important!' She found it hilarious. But local saints are important, because they're ours. Like family, we're stuck with them, which means we're forced to get to know them and discover their deep and hidden qualities. They remind us of the importance of unspectacular lives— lives that are being lived all around us, often invisible from a distance, directly affecting only a few people but indirectly touching many more. Oxfordshire may not be famous for its saints but that doesn't mean there aren't any, or that they don't make a difference.

— ❧ —

Holy Cross

This week sees Ascension Day and the end of the Easter season. It also sees the less widely marked feast of the Invention (in the sense of 'finding') of the Cross. In 326, Helena, mother of the Emperor Constantine, visited Jerusalem and there 'discovered' the cross of Christ. The relic was later captured by the Persians but was recovered again in 629 by the Emperor Heraclitus.

Quite how Helena identified the true cross is understandably vague in ancient accounts, and modern ones are sceptical. But it is worth a thought that Jesus' cross could, in theory, just about still have been around—could only recently have been decommissioned, when Constantine abolished crucifixion after 314. The Romans didn't waste wood making a new cross for everyone they crucified. Jesus' cross had probably been used dozens, if not hundreds, of times before. It was already soaked with the blood and sweat and other bodily fluids of victims, and Jesus' bodily fluids will have soaked into the wood and mingled with those of the victims that came after him.

It symbolises the way Jesus saw his work on earth: to touch; to be in touch; to know by experience. On the cross, he held the traces of all those others as closely to himself as, in life, he had held the sick and outcast, while everyone who hung there after him hung in the imprint of his arms and body, making one body.

We are one body. At the most basic level, we are physically one, made up of the same particles and chemicals and energy. Every being comes together from the worn-out materials of other beings, miraculously re-engineered and resurrected.

Whether we learn it through science or faith or love, we belong together. 'This is my body, which is given for you,' says Jesus,[20] telling us that our life hangs on his death because everyone is connected.

Most of the work of religion lies in appreciating that. So many things disconnect us, set us at odds with each other and create evil, that sure symptom of human estrangement. The cross reminds us of the scale of evil that we have to overcome—the competing desires and fears, the destruction and injustice, the wounds, physical and psychological. But, as Jesus taught, 'You have heard that it was said, "You shall love your neighbour and hate your enemy." But I say to you, love your enemies and pray for those who persecute you, so that you may be children of your Father in heaven; for he makes his sun rise on the evil and on the good, and sends rain on the righteous and on the unrighteous.'[21] This is the text I turn to most often as I grapple with forgiveness, in theory and in practice.

The shape of the Spirit

The Israelites saw the Spirit as a dove. Grey like the clouds from which God spoke to listening hearts, and gentle as rain falling on winter wheat. It had to be sturdy enough to bear an olive branch across a flood, and as light as a blessing descending on a newly baptised head. It was a bird of sacrifice: common, obedient, meek. A bird that mated for life, making it an image of love.

The Celts, on the watery moors and peaks of Caesar's northern empire, saw it as a goose. They guessed how far they were from the centre of the world, and how strong heart and wings must be to bear it all that way. They were grateful to be visited, and proud that their riverbanks and marshes were its breeding grounds. It was an inspiring bird, forging spear-like and dauntless through stormy skies. A bird that travelled in flocks, making it an image of community.

I see the Spirit as a swallow: a shrieking, playful, fearless dart of joy, swooping low over streams and meadows, nesting sociably under the eaves of barns and houses. To us, it is the essence of an English summer, but if you visit Africa in winter, you find it just as much at home swooping over the savannah and playing around the pyramids. It travels where it chooses and we can't hold it, only receive it with gratitude and let it go with grace.

I hear the Spirit as a nightingale. Probably you will never see it but, if you listen long enough in darkness, it may sing to you. No other song is half so varied, so ravishing and resonant. It borrows phrases from every other bird and every other sound, weaves them together and gives them more meaning than they knew they had. While the song lasts, you seem to hear the Spirit singing the song of creation. When it falls silent, you hear creation singing in counterpoint.

The Alice sermon

On Whit Sunday 1862, Charles Dodgson, better known as Lewis Carroll, walked from his Oxford college out to Sandford to preach. In his honour, my father instituted the Alice sermon, which is delivered on Whit Sunday at a festival evensong. I am not a great fan of *Alice in Wonderland*; I don't like the chaotic world she falls into, or the aggression of the characters. My favourite part of the book is the opening scene, on the riverbank at Godstow, where Dodgson has rowed the Liddell sisters up the Thames on a beautiful summer's day.

The riverbank is a kind of heaven: the sun shines and everyone is happy and at peace. The rest of the story is more like life. You fall into it without warning and you never know what's going to happen next. Everyone seems to be in a hurry like the White Rabbit, or indifferent like the Dormouse, or impatient like the Mad Hatter, or just baffling like the Cheshire Cat. Alice deals rather well with everything, even her constantly changing size, but there is a poignant moment when the Caterpillar asks her who she is and she says, 'I hardly know, Sir—at least, I know who I was when I got up this morning, but I think I must have been changed several times since then.' Most of us can sympathise with her bewilderment at some point in our lives.

Alice is haunted by a sense that this is not how the world should be, that things ought to make sense and people ought to be nicer to each other. She longs for something she had forgotten she knew before she fell asleep. From time to time, too, she gets a glimpse of a paradise which she can't reach. At the bottom of the rabbit hole, she finds a tiny door and looks through it into 'the loveliest garden you ever saw'. But first she is too big to get into it, then too small, and then she gets swept away by her own tears. It's 60 pages before Alice reaches that garden, and even then she can't enjoy it because everyone else is too stressed to appreciate it.

That feeling must be, if anything, even more familiar today than when Dodgson wrote it. Whether it's a place, or the company of people we love, or peace with contentment, most of our paradises are lost: either we can't reach them or we have been in them, but didn't realise it at the time. But I also think that Dodgson missed something here. His Alice has plenty of common sense and a strong sense of justice, which help her to break out of Wonderland and get back to her heaven, but she's a bit short on love, which might have helped her make a heaven of where she was.

I am grateful to Dodgson, though, for giving me an image of paradise on that riverbank. We need every glimpse of heaven we can get, or how shall we change the world to reflect it? Giving each other a glimpse of paradise, I reflect, is something we can all do from time to time.

Dodgson's riverbank sets me thinking further about the landscape of heaven. Much as we like to imagine heaven, our images strike me as rather limited. The author of Revelation—influenced by Plato and influencing Augustine—saw it as a city. Some early Christians imagined it as a garden—a new and better Eden. They called it 'paradise' (a word which originally meant a country estate and later a commercial market garden). Others envisaged it as a palace—the 'house with many mansions' of John's Gospel.[22] It all sounds a bit built up to me. Might we not hope for mountains and moors in heaven, forests and lakes—even oceans with islands where only the wind speaks to the waves? As a lover of solitude, I worry about overcrowding, and even more about the emphasis on group activities: singing, feasting, being reunited with everyone we've ever met. Will there be somewhere to go for the people who long just to be alone with God?

There is a Jewish tradition that what God does in heaven is study Torah. Now that I wouldn't mind. If I brush up my Hebrew, perhaps I might be allowed to join the class.

Trinity Sunday

It is Trinity Sunday, and we celebrate with a festival evensong. We have called Oriel chapel choir and they have responded, on the last weekend of their academic year. The Trinity Sunday readings are all stories of people being called: Isaiah, Samuel, Moses and those who, in the book of Proverbs, are seduced by Wisdom into loving God. Some are readier than others, but all respond.

I reflect that we are rarely completely ready. We are beings in transition, creatures of place and time. We're not quite who we were ten years ago and we don't know where we'll be in ten years' time, despite the fact that many of us have a strong sense of who we should be, if life would let us. We long to be more complete; fulfilled. Often it doesn't happen. We spend all our lives coming to be, and then we go without ever having quite arrived.

Perhaps that's why so many of us long for an unchanging God, someone to hold on to in this transitory life. But can we call a God who is sometimes Father and sometimes Son, sometimes flesh and sometimes Spirit, unchanging? Is the God who makes half a dozen different covenants with his people in the course of history wholly unaffected by time and place?

As the choir begins the anthem, it strikes me that our lives are like a piece of music. They start off with a promise of all sorts of things, and gradually they develop and change mood. They have more than one melody, and sometimes they come to a cadence and then go on again. Eventually they end—but however good the ending is, it never contains or justifies the whole piece; too many things have happened on the way.

I imagine God not as a grand perfect cadence waiting for us at the end of the world but as all the music there could ever be. Through time, different parts of it are called into being and harmonise with our lives as they go along. And just as the best piece of music isn't the one with the best ending but the one that's best all through, so the best life is one that goes on developing, becoming part of the slow evolution of eternal life—the joyful, delightful, endlessly creative life of God.

The choir take kindly to having God described as music. After the service, they stay for coffee and chat. 'They're so gifted,' people say with pleasure. What a wonderful thing to sing in a college chapel all the time. Richard, our organist, has given us a taste for quality. On my way home, I reflect that the call to new being doesn't need to find us ready, just present; we may never arrive anywhere much but, if God is already with us, it hardly matters. The main thing is to be part of the music.

The Trinity season

Everyone has their favourite season of the church year, but not many people seem to love the Trinity season. As a child, I found it very dull: more than 20 weeks when nothing happened to speak of and the vestments were always green. A few saints' days, harvest festival and Remembrance Sunday couldn't compare with the excitement of Christmas, Easter and Pentecost.

Nowadays, Trinity is my favourite season, partly because it's summer and I finally get into the garden, which has been disgracefully neglected. There are, I am mortified to discover, thistles in flower in one of the beds. I comfort myself with the thought that the blackbirds raising young in the hedge will have appreciated my absence. A thrush sits on my red fence, scanning the earth for snails. I hear him later, as I sit at my computer, tapping shells to crack them open on the path.

One fine afternoon I cycle to Greater Leys, to see a baby about a baptism. From Littlemore, a lane runs beside the Oxford Academy, under the disused railway line and through the science park. This is starter-home country, conveniently situated close to the football stadium and the multiplex cinema. Amid the modern developments stands a stone house, now a pub, the only remnant of the medieval Mynchery. Even here, thanks to Oxford's green belt, the wind whispers in nearby trees, and there is a rumour of fields just beyond the roundabout. Barely a mile away lie Garsington and the Baldons, villages so lovely that they regularly star in television dramas.

Baptisms tend to come before weddings around here, so much so that I have permanently emended the bit in the wedding service about marriage being the foundation of family life. The first wedding I ever took was of a couple in their mid-30s. They had been together for 20 years and had eight children—the eldest a youth of 18, the youngest a babe in arms. When they decided to tie the knot, all the children acted as bridesmaids and page boys, wearing matching red-and-gold outfits, and after the marriage they thronged the chancel steps like a choir of angels for a blessing. Another couple has just contacted us who, between them, have had seven divorces. 'What do you think?' asks Margreet. 'The triumph of hope?' Whatever we think, I say, the bishop won't let us marry them. They'll have to find a photogenic secular building, of which Oxfordshire, fortunately, has plenty.

One weekend I am given a Sunday off and take the stopping train to Herefordshire. It is the flower of the year. Local stations show off their roses; fields are every shade of green, from silver to lime and beryl to bottle. Two cousins are being christened, Dorothy and Juliet, and their parents have invited all their family and friends. Dorothy's elder sister is my god-daughter Miriam, who has inherited her mother's beauty and musicality. Dorothy looks very like her at the same age. 'We so rarely get together,' says Jessica. 'Better for a baptism than a funeral.' She and Ian, in fact, are amazingly good at getting people together. Somehow they manage to combine two jobs, two children and a huge vegetable garden, with abundant and generous hospitality. In their hands, time seems to expand by being shared.

After the service there is champagne and cake. I don't know many of the other guests so I sneak out to take a walk around the churchyard. On the way I pass a small boy who has found a picture book of Gospel stories and wants to take it home. 'I don't know what you want a book for,' says his mother irritably. 'You don't even feed your rabbit.'

Outside, fat clouds scurry sheepishly before a snapping wind. Other members of the discreet fellowship of the shy are here: one or two adults and a few children, scouting among the graves or playing in the rose garden. Someone catches my eye and smiles. There is more than one way to be a community. A stressed father, stalking down the path, snaps to his son, 'Don't be so antisocial! Get back in there!' and heads for his car. The son looks miserable (may Juliet and Dorothy never look so sad). One of the other children, inspired, invites him to play.

At lunch I sit near the vicar, who tells me that although Herefordshire farmers have been hard hit in recent years, there is great optimism among the young. They plan to economise, diversify, expand local markets—whatever it takes to keep working the land. Children dash, squealing excitedly, among the guests. It is a good day to be hopeful.

In summer, people can find time to be baptised, to marry, to weed the garden; above all, to stop and think about the past few months. There is a lot to ponder. Did we see enough of friends and family? Did we pray enough, give enough thanks? The Collect for the third Sunday of Trinity asks God to help us, 'to whom thou hast given an hearty desire to pray'. Being given a hearty desire to pray is one of the many things for which I am grateful in summer. St Augustine thought he knew why we had it: 'Lord, you have made us for yourself alone, and our hearts are restless till they find their rest in you.' [23]

— ❦ —

Valerian

A remarkable thing has happened in my garden. I wanted to grow some valerian, that pretty summer perennial with pink or white flowers. I had been told that it would grow anywhere so, when I saw a local school wall thick with self-seeded plants, I picked a few. (In a possibly misdirected fit of conscience, I did this on a Sunday so as not to set a bad example to the children.) I didn't get many roots but I planted the stems and watered them—and one by one they died. The flowers went mouldy, the leaves fell off and the stems turned black and brittle.

I left them there anyway, thinking that maybe, if I was lucky, the roots would take and send up new shoots next spring. I was completely unprepared for what happened. After several weeks of being dead, the stems began to turn green again from the bottom up. Slowly the greenness climbed from joint to joint. New leaves sprouted. One or two are even trying to flower. I wouldn't have believed it if I hadn't seen it. But I have heard that if you plant planks made of willow, they will root and sprout and turn back into trees, and now I can believe that. You can't overestimate the power of life.

One of my valerian shoots has not revived, and I think it really is dead. But I regret it less because of the others. Not because it doesn't matter in itself—it does—but because to die in a world where life is so vigorous and miracles happen is very different from dying in a world where miracles never happen and death always wins. The world we leave behind us bristles with resurrections.

Sandra, a local funeral director, rings me about a funeral

next week. The dead man wanted his wife to be able to visit him easily, so they booked a plot for his ashes in the churchyard, but, not being churchgoers, they didn't want a religious service. Sandra told them firmly that if they wanted the churchyard they had to have a priest, and I'm it. I go round to the house, admiring its immaculate garden—the lawn freshly mowed, the pergola over the gate laden with roses. Twenty members of the immediate family and several large dogs are there to interview me as I talk to the widow. I am cravenly tempted to assure her that I'll make it as secular as possible... but I think of Sandra, and resist.

Four hundred people turn up at the crematorium; the crowd mills round the doorway of the chapel and listens to the service via loudspeakers. Family members come up one by one and tell vivid stories of Tony—patriarch, fish-monger, lorry driver, scaffolder, sportsman, dog show judge, motorcyclist, snooker player, friend, great man. I keep the prayers short and everyone joins in. Afterwards, a few of the more religious members of the congregation stop to talk. 'He was a marvellous man,' they say. 'It's a shame you didn't know him.' You never know everyone, even in a small parish; I often bury people I wish I'd known. The glimpses I get of them through their family and friends fill me with wonder.

— ❧ —

Two church fêtes

Littlemore is unfortunate in lacking the sort of village green where you can hold a fête. There is the triangle outside the chip shop, but it is small, sloping and bounded by busy roads. There are a couple of playground spaces on the edge of the village, but they are right next to the bypass. So we have our parish fêtes in the village hall or the community centre. Both are well placed and roomy, but you could not call them beautiful. For a summer idyll, one must walk up the road to Sandford.

The Sandford fête takes place on the playing field beside the church. There are stalls selling tea and cakes and books and plants; lucky dips and bouncy castles and a tug of war; hot dogs and cold beer. Inside a corral of parked pushchairs, 16 drum majorettes twizzle and stamp to Girls Aloud. Small children amble past with painted faces: tigers and eagles and butterflies licking ice creams. It is an afternoon to bump into people one hasn't seen for ages, to picnic on the grass, and to spend money lavishly and, if possible, without acquiring too much to carry home.

Indoor games are the rule at Littlemore, and a most reliable way to lose money. I am equally bad at shove ha'penny, treasure-hunting and guessing the number of sweets in a jar. When a law was passed banning the sale of cakes made in unlicensed kitchens, the fête conformed for a year, registered with dismay a dramatic drop in profits, and opted for civil disobedience in the future. Jean's strawberry jam goes in the back of the fridge until midwinter, when one spoonful will bring summer flooding back. I man the jewellery stall for a while with Nancy, who has turned out her drawers to stock it. Every piece has a story. Six painted wooden buttons were brought back from Austria by her late husband, who took a water polo team from Malta on tour there at the end of the Second World War. They and their story will look handsome on a green cardigan.

Strolling between heaped trestles, I reflect on the parallels between fêtes and the miracle of the loaves and fishes. We start with almost nothing, and everyone brings a little and buys and plays a little until, astonishingly, at the end of the afternoon, we have not only made enough money to tide us over the next few months, but there are twelve baskets of unsold bric-a-brac left over.

On the road

The road between my house and the church climbs one of the steep hills which ring the Oxford basin. If I am in a hurry or want a workout, I take the main road up Rose Hill. In winter the air is sharp and disputatious; in summer the sun rests on the brow of the hill and dazzles me. If I have more time, I take green and sheltered Meadow Lane, which follows the river up through Iffley village.

Winter and summer, early and late, this twelve-minute cycle ride acts as a kind of decompression chamber. I leave home—sometimes late, sometimes irritable, often unprepared—and, without thinking of anything much on the journey, I arrive ready to pray.

Twenty to eight, in winter, finds me trying to light damp candles with damp matches and not looking forward to taking off my coat. Any warmth from last Thursday evening's service has long since seeped out of the chancel. Dawn makes little impression on the dark stained glass. For no obvious reason, at this moment I am always happy. The vestry is colder, if possible, than the church; the silver chalice and paten freeze to my fingers. I always wonder whether anyone will turn out, and half a dozen always do.

One summer morning, a stranger appeared at the eight o'clock service. He explained that he was visiting from South Africa, looking up family connections in Littlemore. 'I feel sorry for you,' he said. 'Where I come from, there would be 200 people at a morning service.' I felt faintly guilty that I did not long for a larger congregation at my Prayer Book Communion, but I don't. I love the quietness of it. Those who come pray deeply, and power goes out from them into the streets around. They are long-time neighbours, exchanging a few words afterwards from the middles of on-going conversations. In summer we leave the door open, and I give the final blessing to sunlit grass and thrushes. I note that Sue's Christmas tree cross, which she reckoned would get knocked down by vandals before Easter, is still upright in the churchyard three months later.

Sometimes the journey to church is longer and less familiar. As a non-stipendiary minister, I am clerical poly-filla: any church that is stuck for a celebrant can call me in. One summer Sunday, I am whisked off in a car (rare treat) to Kingston Bagpuize, where a large and charismatic congregation worships in a small neo-classical church. You don't expect to find a gem of Regency architecture in an Oxfordshire village, but the medieval church burned down in 1800 and was rebuilt in the fashion of the day. Now it sits amid woodland and cottage gardens, looking very chic and slightly self-conscious, like a cocktail dress at a coffee morning. Kingston Bagpuize is between vicars, and the con-gregation has risen to the challenge, alternating Eucharists with lay-led worship. The lay-led services, I am told, attract even more people than the conventional ones. In interregna, congregations often discover among themselves a wealth of gifts they did not know they had.

Another Sunday finds me catching the London bus before dawn to help Bernhard out at South Dulwich. Greater love hath no former curate than this, I think blearily, as I mark changes to my sermon and the bus ploughs along the dark M40. In Oxfordshire, NSMs used to be called 'auxiliaries', after the second-class troops of the Roman army. Now we are known as 'associates', after the subjects of the Roman Empire. I like being non-stipendiary, and I always enjoy my visits to other parishes, but I worry that using NSMs as dioceses do, to plug gaps among the stipendiary clergy, rather than as a resource in their own right, obscures the extent to which the parish system—like the Roman Empire—depends on its associates. And that (despite the occasional lip-service paid to 'Fresh Expressions of church') encourages dioceses to avoid difficult questions about how parishes will survive, and how they must change, if paid clergy decline further in numbers. In the coming years, I suspect, more parish priests will have other jobs, and members of congregations will do even more in church. Rather than considering this as a crisis and a change forced on us by circumstances, I should rather see us embrace the opportunity to become more like our earliest forebears—a community in which everyone has an active and properly valued role, a priesthood of all believers.

However short or long, the journey to church is always forgotten in the pleasure of arriving. It is good to see old friends and catch up with their news. At Dulwich, Bernhard has persuaded Nicholas Ansdell-Evans to write a grand organ fanfare for their patronal festival.

John Henry Newman

Littlemore is a parish of two halves, in more senses than one. There are the council estates, and the gated apartments carved out of the old psychiatric hospital. There is the present, in which Littlemore is an unpretentious suburb, and history, in which it is famous because John Henry Newman built our church and, round the corner, established 'The College', the community to which he retired from Oxford to study with a hand-picked group of young men.

We don't think about John Henry much from week to week, though pilgrims sometimes visit the church and, at the bicentenary of his birth, we hosted a grand ecumenical service. Arvo Pärt was commissioned to write an anthem to Newman's words, and great men of all denominations came to show off their Oxford Movement connections. We do, however, have an illegal icon of Newman in his cardinal's robes (illegal because only saints are supposed to be shown on icons and Newman is not a saint in the Orthodox Church), and we joke that if he is sanctified, we may finally make some money. We plan to turn the vicar's garage into a visitors' centre-cum-tearoom and display Newman's vestments and the framed autograph of 'Lead kindly light' which used to hang on the vestry wall. Nancy's son Tom wonders where you get those little figurines made, with the haloes that light up.

The College is a converted stables, a low stone building hugging the corner opposite the Blue Mile pub. Through its front gate, you step into another world. A bust of John Henry stands wreathed in rosemary in the courtyard garden. It gleams quietly in the evening light as a group of us pace past, along the cloister. The College is beautifully maintained nowadays by the Catholic Sisters of the Work, and the library's polished floor, white book-lined walls and engravings lend our discussion group an air of distinction. A couple of years ago, the Archbishop of Canterbury came to a conference here and, at the end of his stay, celebrated the Eucharist in church. A specially designed hassock (Elo's sketch of Newman's kindly light shining over the church tower, stitched by Mo in black wool) commemorates the occasion. It sits under the priest's stall, so anyone who celebrates now kneels under Newman's pulpit on the legend, '+ Rowan in Littlemore, 2005'. If that doesn't induce humility, I think, as I settle on to creaking knees, what would? The members of the congregation re-member the Archbishop affectionately in their prayers, and follow his activities with interest.

As I was locking up the church after the eight o'clock service one morning, a stranger appeared and asked to be let in. He'd timed his arrival, he explained blandly, for the end of the service, so he could look around. Suppressing a tart rejoinder, I unlocked the door again. The visitor came from Withyham in Sussex, whose church, commissioned by a Victorian lady of the manor who was a fan of the Oxford Movement, is a copy of ours. It is not alone: Llangorwen near Aberystwyth, Roehampton, and Littleworth, just up the road near Faringdon, also have churches based on ours. Grandest of all, the cathedral church of St Mark in George, South Africa, began life as plain St Mark's church and a copy of Littlemore. I meditate on the vicissitudes of fame as I wait for the gentleman from Withyham to finish taking photographs.

— ❦ —

Flower festival

Sandford is hosting its flower festival, choral evensong and the 'green sermon', the parish's annual eco-theological event. July sun streams in at the south windows of the church, turning it into a bowl of·light. This year's theme is 'Books of the Bible', and on every side, marvels of sculpted colour dazzle the eye: lilies piled on delphiniums, carnations bursting from beds of fern, lacy gypsophila dancing over dark palm leaves. The air is as damp as a greenhouse and heavy with pollen. Since Littlemore only occasionally holds a flower festival, some of our keenest arrangers 'show' at Sandford. They remember that before our church was built, Littlemore people came to Sandford, it being more their style than the University Church and just down the road. Liz—architect, lay reader and expert gardener—has written a history of the church, which is on display for visitors to buy.

To some people, flowers evoke such wonder that they seem to prove God's existence or illustrate God's nature. Others feel the force that forms the flower running through our veins: building our bones, drawing the skin over our flesh, making us walk and think and hope and love. We cannot see the force and we may never understand it, but we sense that we embody it, express and communicate it.

An amateur like me can only guess how much work goes into our weekly flower arrangements in Littlemore. At Christmas and Easter they become works of high art, framing statues, scaling the pulpit and wreathing the font and candlesticks. Flowers in church are like angels—messengers from heaven that remind us of glories we can't see. Like saints and sacraments, they help us encounter God through our different senses.

After evensong, I visit my grandparents' grave in Sandford churchyard. Sitting crosslegged at the end of their plot, as in childhood I used to sit on the end of their bed, I rest my hands on the green counterpane. The flesh whose flesh created mine is part of the earth now. This earth created me. 'Make the most of life,' it seems to say. 'All flesh is as grass, and all the glory of man as the flower of grass.'[24]

Pilgrimages

I take a walk to Kilpeck in Herefordshire, that exquisite Norman church with its unique mixture of Saxon, Viking, Celtic, Frankish and Spanish decoration. There's no particular occasion, except that it is summer. I have a pleasing sense of breaking bounds—of setting off, as we sometimes need to do, to find God in the sanctuary of strangers.

On either side of the country roads, the fields have been stripped of their cloth of gold, and stand untidily thatched with living straw. From time to time, as I approach a village, a spire rears through the cumulus of trees to engrave questions on the air. Why are we here? Is this the way to heaven?

It is hot and heavy high summer, a time for sitting in the shade or lying on mown grass, gleaning time, redeeming time. I reach Kilpeck's round pre-Christian churchyard and flop down in the shade to eat sandwiches and take a nap. Over the years I have fallen asleep in more churchyards than I can remember. I dream of dancing on a heat wave, slipping the cogs of mind and body. Hours spread out like leaves to skim the cream of summer. On its modest hummock of ground, the church looks over flattish farmland towards the ridge of the Black Mountains. Other visitors arrive in cars and dart like bees into the gloom, hoping to bag its sweetness before driving on to Herefordshire's next architectural flower.

Later, clouds form, the afternoon sun sinks and the wind shifts uneasily. 'Remember,' it whispers, 'autumn is coming.' I slip into the church on a spatter of rain and climb the stony aisle towards the tiny apsidal chancel. The dust of long-dead worshippers filters down from the rafters and mingles familiarly with my own. Before I reach the altar, I know that it hardly matters whether or not I arrive. What I have come to seek is already with me.

Back home, Brenda is planning a different kind of pilgrimage. Cardinal House is being pulled down and she must leave her flat, home for 18 years, for a smaller, less attractive and more distant one in another warden-assisted block. Most of all, she will miss the view over Newman Road, the children walking to and from school, the sunsets. 'You don't expect a lot more surprises,' she says, 'in your 80s', but God has always got another challenge for her. She is determined to rise to it. Someone will be grateful for the clothes she sends to the charity shop. Letting go of most of her furniture will remind her of her first married home, where she and Harry made do with a table, a desk, two chairs, and a china cabinet which their predecessor couldn't face carrying downstairs. With St Paul, Brenda believes that suffering ultimately leads to hope, and hope does not disappoint us. I am reminded of another wise man, Solon of Athens, who said, 'I grow old always learning many things.'[25] Brenda will go on learning, and teaching the rest of us, for as long as her pilgrimage lasts.

The church in the middle of nowhere

I built this church
in case you should be lost
and need a lookout or a lode
or a fistful of air
so magnetised to God that you would know,
opening, it is the place love leads all roads.

We're close here to the watershed. Wrinkles
of limestone shift to catch the running snow
on its April migration to the sea.
An apple core that someone threw away
blossoms, and there are vines, somewhere
a pruning hook. It is no mystery

but everywhere I go
myths of a mountain Eden, where the world
fell into place around your feet
burgeon. Many tell stories. Fewer lose
themselves to find the path. So lifetimes pass
on the rich plains of wisdom. The church waits.

Neighbours

I drop in on Nancy and we sit on her veranda, under a vine laden with picturesque though inedible bunches of grapes, and drink tea. We talk about travel, past and planned, and books and writing projects. 'Where are you going next?' Nancy wants to know. Italy, Finland, America? She is much better travelled than I am and, being a modern linguist, better equipped too. At the moment, however, we are both confined to time travel: Nancy is writing up some of her family's history and I am writing about the Romans.

The ancient willow tree in Nancy's garden whips snaky branches in the breeze, like a cross between the green man and Medusa. I think of willows as friendly beings, coming into leaf before any other big tree and falling only at the beginning of Advent. Nancy prefers the magnolia next door. In a built-up area, one best appreciates one's neighbours' trees, which add colour and texture to the street without dropping their leaves where one has to rake them up.

My favourite local trees are nine flat-headed, wide-branched, snow-white cherries, which screen an unpretentious block of flats at the top of Rose Hill. Iffley churchyard has a single venerable pink cherry, which I also visit ritually each spring. Last October I picked up a few of its leaves which had fallen before the frost, palettes of yellow and green dabbled with red. Lying all winter in my fireplace, they gradually turned crimson all over. In April I took them back and laid them carefully on the grass, where they looked like an omen of next year's leaves, aged and fallen before they had been born. Time zoomed madly back and forth for a few moments and, gratified, I left the leaves there for other visitors.

In John and Helen's garden, as seen through the window of their dining room, certain plants and shrubs mark the progress of the Bible study group through the year. In my mind's eye, the book of Daniel is forever bordered with snowdrops; 1 Corinthians smells of roses; Romans is the purple of Michaelmas daisies. We read the text aloud, chapter by chapter, savouring the language. Beryl and the two Jeans have a flair for the dramatic and often capture a hint of comedy lurking below the surface of a story. Jean's Bible is her family one, Judy's a study edition; Helen's was a christening present. Between us we have five translations, which spark discussions of meaning and consultation of the original. I enthuse about history. Judy is the theologian among us. John listens benignly as the women talk. Stories lead to reminiscences and reflections on our own lives. We have also learned not to be afraid of silences.

In hospital

It is a universal truth of parish life that there is always at least one person in hospital. Several members of our congregation are frequent visitors to the various strongholds of the NHS which squat like pillboxes around the shoulders of Headington Hill. Joan, though, is not, so when I arrive on the ward she tries to find me a chair and regrets that she can't offer me a cup of tea. 'Look at the view!' she says, and we stand for a moment admiring the distant green quilt of Otmoor, like a couple of tourists newly arrived at a foreign hotel.

On another floor Ella wishes she could see the city centre, which, at 98, she fears she will never walk round again. Her family was in service in the Judge's lodgings, and her father played the last post at Oxford's very first Armistice Day celebration. A lifelong churchgoer, Ella is preparing for death by recalling her shortcomings over the years and asking forgiveness for them. She has lost her false teeth, and they have brought her some from home which are 50 years old and fit her mouth as it was then, not as it is now. It's disconcerting, she says—like going back, when she's trying to go forward. It's made her realise that the process of decay is very long and piecemeal. Some parts of us die before others. Others go on growing after what the present state of science defines as the moment of death. The process isn't all one way, either: since coming into hospital, Ella says, she's put on weight and in some ways she thinks she looks younger.

Paul is very close to death. He holds my hand through the bars of his bed. 'Are you comfortable?' he asks periodically. 'Are the bars hurting you? I hope I'm not boring you.' He needs to talk because, among all these strangers who know him only as a bundle of diseases, he is afraid that he is losing the person he has been, even while his body is still alive. As he talks, he recovers himself.

Walking from one wing of the hospital to another, I reflect that we spend too much time aspiring to perfection of mind and body. The greatest beauty, the fastest runner, the prize-winning artist of the moment are lauded and lionised. Everyone else—which is almost everyone—feels inadequate by comparison, and the best becomes the enemy of the good. But not even the best are perfectly wise or eternally beautiful, and to be imperfect, to age and sicken and die are natural and universal. To deny it or to rage against it are equally pointless and destructive. We do better when we embrace our ever-changing nature, imperfection as well as perfection, decay as well as growth, death as well as birth, as part of the way God wants us to be.

I start thinking of reasons why we should thank God for decay and death. Because the very power of the life which runs through us wears out our bodies and minds, while through death our atoms and energies are reused and we become part of new lives. Because life, being limited, has shape, tension and trajectory: knowing we will die—if not in a fort-night, then some day—concentrates our minds. Because each generation, giving place to the next, makes possible endless diversity of experience, progress and change. Because death reminds us that we are not the measure of all things.

The hospital, paradoxically, is not an easy place in which to meditate on change and decay, not only because it battles against them but because it forms its own ecosystem—a world without seasons, heat or cold, rain or drought. Even night and day become blurred. I step through the front doors into a blast of August heat and freewheel down the hill with the sun on my neck, grateful that, for now at least, I am going home.

Michaelmas

The feast of St Michael and All Angels heralds the beginning of the academic year. Oxford is beautiful in the autumn, with its horse chestnuts turning gold and cherry trees aflame. They are digging up the High Street, so I have ample time to admire the scenery as I queue for the roundabout. The children, of course, have been back at school for nearly a month. They overtake me on the pavement, very blasé in rumpled uniforms and artfully scuffed shoes. In college, the hall steps are lined with scarlet geraniums in pots, which look extremely smart, like a parade of very small grenadier guards.

From my stately book-lined room over the main gate, I look out over Oriel Square and into the front quad. There is nearly always something interesting to see but, at the beginning of term, I am too busy meeting students to spend time looking out. The only student who doesn't appear has caught mumps. Oriel, our doctors tell us, is the epicentre of a university-wide outbreak. This is a result of the MMR scare, which caused a generation of children not to be vaccinated. The doctors have been urging students not to kiss each other till the epidemic is over, but they seem to prefer to have both kissing and mumps.

The recession, meanwhile, infects everyone. The college considers how to economise. 'I'll eat Marmite sandwiches every day,' says one young Fellow fiercely, 'as long as I can keep my research allowance.' At the same time, the leak in the chancel roof of the University Church can no longer be ignored and, as patron, the college is responsible for patching it up. Chancel roofs, it transpires, are not cheap. It is out of the question to cut the teaching budget and no one wants to increase student rents, so the economies will have to be elsewhere. The Treasurer is sent away to come up with ideas.

Angels are the unofficial patrons not only of new academic years, but of new beginnings of all kinds. The first time they appear in the Bible is when God casts Adam and Eve out of Eden to begin their new life. It is angels who announce to Abraham the birth of his son and the beginning of the people of Israel, and an angel who proclaims the incarnation to Mary. In the parish, we celebrate Michaelmas with the wonderful Methodist Covenant Service. 'Christ has many services to be done,' we say:

Some are easy, others are difficult;
some bring honour, others bring reproach;
some suit our natural inclinations and material interests,
others are contrary to both;
in some we may please Christ and please ourselves,
in others we cannot please Christ except by denying ourselves.
Yet the power to do all these things is given to us in Christ,
who strengthens us.

Eternal God, in your faithful and enduring love
you call us to share in your gracious covenant in Jesus Christ.
In obedience we hear and accept your commands;
in love we seek to do your perfect will;
with joy we offer ourselves anew to you.
We are no longer our own but yours.

I am no longer my own but yours.
Your will, not mine, be done in all things, wherever you may
place me,
in all that I do and in all that I may endure;
when there is work for me and when there is none;

when I am troubled and when I am at peace.
Your will be done when I am valued and when I am disregarded;
when I find fulfilment and when it is lacking;
when I have all things and when I have nothing.
I willingly offer all that I have and am to serve you, as and where
                                                              you choose.

This is one of those rare pieces of modern liturgy that say exactly what I want to say, in beautiful and inspiring language.

In my sermon I question whether we really need heavenly beings to carry messages between us and God. What's wrong with speaking to God directly? Nothing—and we can and do it all the time. In the same spirit, we don't really *need* saints. But sometimes, for whatever reason, we can all do with a bit of extra help. Someone a little more like ourselves to set us an example. A being who reminds us that we are close to God when we don't feel close; that we are made in God's image when it doesn't look like it; that whatever happens to us, we are still and always loved by God. Stories and experiences of angels and saints do that. Sometimes, too, we do it for each other.

We shall need to do it more often in the months ahead. The recession is hitting us all, one way or another. There are redundancies at the car works, both the Blue Mile and the Fox at Sandford have gone out of business, and we shall struggle to pay our parish share. At the Gentlemen's Breakfast, I hear, the men have been discussing whether a society without manufacturing can maintain its self-respect or consider itself to be on a sound economic footing. The gentlemen (who meet once a month in the village hall for a full English fry-up) are inclined to think that it cannot. They then look around and realise that, of those present, not one is in manufacturing.

Guardian angels come in all shapes and sizes. We have a new one in the form of Sainsbury's supermarket on the ring-road, which has started to give the church some of the flowers it hasn't sold at the end of each week. The ingenuity of the flower-arranging team is tested by some of the combinations they receive. They could write a book, they say: *Days of Pine and Roses* or *101 Carnations*.

Conversations with angels

I

Happiness
for angels
is to stand
fast over the thermals of your prayers
while light
glances off scarcely ruffling wings
to pierce your downcast eyes.

Thank you
for your warm words;
for letting your hopes rise.

II

I saw you dancing
earlier today: the city squirmed
in ecstasy beneath your tickling feet.
Radcliffe's Camera rocked on cobbled seas
and all its railings rippled in the breeze.
You made the street lamps fizz and sprayed
doves like champagne over triumphal treetops;
Cherwell lay green-bellied while you stroked her
with willow-shade.

Who me?

I saw you dancing, don't pretend you didn't
every time the apex of my needle lost itself in
admiration, and on the mantel sweet peas braced
their heads to take the weight of happiness.

III

Do you ever wonder
what I'm like?

I see you as a mirror, in which I catch
myself in unexpected poses, and the world around
at angles I had not thought about;
and if I'm lucky, every now and then
you bend on me a ray of that elusive light
by which I see, whose heat sustains my breath,
but which I cannot turn to face
this side of death.

IV

Where are you when I need you?
Here.

Give me a sign, if you exist.
My arms are round you.

V

I am the echo of your voice returning
to reassure you there is something
there for your words to resonate against.

I am the echo
sometimes that you surprise yourself by making
of voices you did not know you heard.

I am the sounding-board
on which one day you will recognize you are
an echo of something far more resonant.

VI

Will you be with me always? *One day*
you will stand face to face with God.

Will you be there?
Yes, like your shadow where the sun falls on it.

VII

I thought it was the swallows flying south.
A crowd of wings waved madly
as black handkerchiefs on the horizon:
Goodbye, remember us! Then one and then a dozen
shoals breasting below the bright flotilla
of icy clouds that cruised the arctic sky.

I thought it was the swallows leaving us with the
                                        September light
then they passed over
and the air leapt and fractured—turbid,
brilliant with angels, and the shining
swept us along and up and in and there was no such thing
                                        as night.

Harvest Festival

I head for Leicestershire again at what townies think of as harvest time, though harvesting of one kind or another has been going on since June. I tramp the field paths, finding new vistas on the best-trodden routes. In winter, this is prime hunting country, with its low hills, shallow valleys and well-kept hedges. In autumn, tractors and trailers dominate. The villages, which even in my childhood were mostly working communities, are now mostly dormitories for commuters, but the farmers are still here.

At this time of year, Leicestershire is a glimpse of Eden. The gold that shone a few weeks ago on freshly combined fields now touches the trees. The earth breaks in brown waves where ploughs turn the stubble. Ridge and furrow point down to a village hidden in a fold of ground and up to an ancient road. If you stop at any high point and look west and south towards Warwickshire and Northamptonshire, you can pretend that the landscape of fields, hedges and occasional church towers stretches all the way to the sea.

Back home, October roots the last warmth out of the sheltered corners of the garden. Chairs and gardening tools and toys for visiting children, which camped outside during the hot weeks of summer, develop an uneasy, displaced look. Eventually I take pity and tidy them away. I have chopped back the sea-blue ceanothus, which arched like an umbrella over the garden path and blocked out half the light. Stepping out of the kitchen door now, I can see so much more sky that it's like a new garden. I muse on the relationship between heaven and earth. The solid here-and-now of green and brown is more miraculous as we contemplate its origin and end in blue infinity. The sun shines from deep space on to my flower beds, and they are one.

There isn't much warmth in the sun, though. I retreat indoors to make tea. The garden is left to stray roses and fat harvest spiders, who throw up more and more acrobatic nets to catch the last few flies.

'You crown the year with Your goodness,' says the Collect for Harvest Festival, and then reminds us to check that friends and neighbours are also prepared for the coming winter. 'You give us the fruits of the earth in season: grant that we may use them… for the relief of those in need.'

These days, the fruits of the earth need to be bottled, tinned or dried. On the Saturday morning before harvest festival, I pant up the hill with a rattling basketful and add them to the piles growing in the chancel. This is also our 'Harvest of talents' weekend. Some of the pews have been boarded over and villagers are bringing displays of paintings, sculptures, poetry, flower arrangements, knitwear, crochet, basket-weaving, pottery and any and every creative thing they do.

A highlight is Andrew's panoramic photographs of places his family have visited on holiday in France. One of these includes the Canadian memorial at the Vimy Ridge. On Saturday afternoon, a visitor from Canada passes the church, walks casually in and sees the photograph of the memorial. His grandfather, who had fought there, was at the memorial's unveiling, and the man himself had visited it that year for the first time. Overwhelmed, he arranges to buy the photograph from Andrew at the end of the exhibition. Judith, whom I have not met before, brings a book she has bound and embossed, and some astonishing photographs of light. As she chats to Margreet, it emerges that she is also a singer and she is persuaded to join the singing group. Casting a critical eye over our battered lectionary and altar book, she offers to rebind them in leather. There are CDs on sale of Rachel singing arias and Richard conducting the Oxford Girls' Choir.

After church on Sunday, we join up with the Baptist and Catholic congregations for a bring-and-share harvest lunch. On the loaves and fishes principle, there is far too much to eat. The generosity of the community mirrors the generosity of God, and the fruits of the kitchen make visible, and edible, the fruit of the Spirit. I drift home lethargically, almost too full to pedal. Fat drops of rain fall around me, speckling the tarmac and cooling the air. At home, I collapse on the sofa with a groan. When I wake up around teatime, the rain has stopped and a robin that only visits my garden in winter is rooting for worms under the sodden geraniums.

St Frideswide

Frideswide is an autumnal sort of saint, quiet and unflashy. According to her biographers, she was born towards the end of the seventh century, the daughter of a Saxon king of Oxford. She consecrated herself a virgin but King Algar of Leicester wanted to marry her, so, to avoid him, she was transported miraculously to the nearby village of Bampton, or possibly to Binsey. Frideswide remained in hiding for three years, keeping pigs. Algar tried to force his way into Oxford and was killed in the attempt.

Local legend tells a slightly different story. While Frideswide was still a princess, Algar tried to rape her and was struck blind by lightning as a punishment. Frideswide prayed to St Margaret of Antioch and a well sprang up at Binsey in answer to her prayers. She bathed Algar's eyes in the water and he regained his sight but accepted that she was not for him. Frideswide founded a nunnery in the centre of Oxford, spent the rest of her life there in peace and died around 730.

I envisage Frideswide growing up in a privileged environment and finding that it didn't suit her. Realising that there's more to life than making a good marriage, and that meaning can't be measured in jewellery and livestock. Slowly she fell in love with something the world couldn't give her. As a princess, she won't have been seduced by images of God as king, the power and the glory. She went to make life in a small plain house, trusting that the God who made everything would forgive her for not wanting most of it.

This year, Frideswide's feast (19 October) falls on a Sunday. In preparation, I decide to cycle to the three places where she lived and worked, to pay my respects. From home to the centre of town is an easy ride along the river. In Christ Church, sadly, there is little to commemorate Oxford's patron saint. The cathedral was built over her nunnery. Only a side chapel preserves her very bare shrine, with a large but rather confusing window showing scenes from her life.

Bampton is about ten miles to the west—out of town on the Botley Road, round the reservoir where a few hardy souls are still windsurfing, past the newly restored stone circle at Stanton Harcourt, over the Windrush and down through Hardwick and Aston. The villages round here are pretty and prosperous, benefiting once from Cotswold wool and now from fast road and rail links to London. The parish church at Bampton has Saxon foundations, but the only memorial of Frideswide is a picture in the window of another side chapel, where she appears holding a bunch of lilies and accompanied by a pig.

From there I return to Binsey, against the flow of Saturday afternoon traffic inching out of the city. Time was when pilgrimages *were* the traffic round here. Binsey-on-Thames, on Oxford's northern edge, was once one of the great pilgrimage sites of England. King Henry VIII brought Katherine of Aragon here to pray for a son. Now, I reflect, as I pant back down the Botley Road, pilgrims of any faith are travelling against the flow, not just of the traffic but of our whole culture, and Binsey is a tiny church down an obscure lane. When I arrive, however, a helpful pamphlet tells me about Frideswide and explains why the church is dedicated to St Margaret of Antioch. The well is still there, well tended. In the Middle Ages, any healing fluid was called a 'treacle', and Binsey well is the treacle well of *Alice's Adventures in Wonderland*. Alice and her sisters probably knew it, as their governess came from Binsey.

So Frideswide has her wish for obscurity. I admire her—

a woman of peace, unstoppable in her vocation; a practical as well as a spiritual person; a woman who demanded and got respect in a man's world; a woman of more compassion and more vision than those who thought they owned her. Before I leave Binsey, I say a prayer for the city and all who live and work here. Outside, I look into Frideswide's well and ask for some of her unfussy holiness to stick to all of us as we walk the ground she walked.

All Saints and All Souls

It is a day of wrath in the garden. Gusts of wind strip the trees of leaves, which raise skeletal hands in supplication towards an indifferent sky. Rain billows and breaks in waves over my red fence. Crouching in the lee of the larch tree, I cut down a burned-out display of giant alliums. Their bulbs rest in the dark earth, waiting faithfully for the trumpet-call of spring.

We are poised between All Saints and All Souls, a pair of festivals almost as different from each other as Good Friday and Easter Day. In church, we celebrate All Saints in the morning; in the evening, we keep All Souls with our annual service for those who have lost friends or family.

All Saints, I reflect, is an unusual festival—what one might call a 'bottom up' festival. Rather than celebrating what God has given us, it remembers what thousands of remarkable people have given God. It is also an encouraging festival because saints, however holy, are also recognisably like ourselves. They come from all walks of life. Some are learned and some illiterate, some joyful and some serious, some peaceful and some troublemakers. There are as many ways to be saintly as there are saints, and as many paths into the kingdom of heaven as there are people who tread them.

One day, perhaps, one of those paths will be ours. The New Testament is optimistic: the Greek *hagios*, 'holy' or 'saint', is also the word which writers from Paul onwards use for all Christians. We are all saints—if not yet, then in the making! We all hope and pray to be transformed, to be lit up by faith like a November bonfire.

But will we manage it? From the first days, the hope of holiness has been entwined in Christian hearts with fear—of temptation and of our own imperfect natures. At All Souls we pray for the faithful departed, but the mood of All Souls is much darker than that of All Saints and its most famous hymn is not the triumphant 'For all the saints...' but the fearful *Dies Irae*:[26]

Day of wrath, that day will dissolve the earth in ashes as David and the Sybil prophesied.
What trembling there will be when the Judge shall come to judge all things in strictness.
A trumpet, sounding its wonderful note through the graves of every land, will drive mankind before the throne.

Praying for the dead, we end up praying for ourselves, for we shall all be dead one day. And what will the judgment be on us?

What then shall I say, wretch that I am, what advocate entreat to speak for me, when even the righteous may hardly be safe?
I groan like a guilty man. Guilt reddens my face. Spare a suppliant, O God.

Even to imagine coming face to face with God is terrifying, but the writer reminds us that we do not do it on our own. Between us and the king stands Christ. We put our trembling, fragile, all-too-imperfect lives into his hands.

I pray in supplication on my knees, my heart as contrite as the dust, safeguard my end.

Just before sunset the wind drops, the clouds grow thin and gauzy and the sky is suffused with gold. The heavens are not so much being torn open as melting into the arms of the reclining sun. Outside the kitchen window, a spider, undeterred by the wild weather and the complete absence of insects, begins a new web.

I venture out once more, picking my way between saturated shrubs, to cut a couple of late rosebuds which have survived the tempest. 'What are you doing, flowering in November?' I mutter as I arrange them with sprigs of rosemary on the mantelpiece. 'Why not flower?' they seem to say. 'God may come at any time. We want to be ready, doing what we do best.' It strikes me that it isn't so very long till Advent. Oh, not yet! The roses may be ready, but I am not.

Fun Church

One Sunday event I rarely manage to attend is Fun Church, which takes place at four o'clock in the afternoon, every other week in the village hall. This week, for once, I have made it, together with about 15 children under the age of seven and a gaggle of parents and grandparents. We sit in concentric circles, most of the children and Margreet crosslegged on the floor; adults, babies and the more restless children on chairs. Sometimes a child takes off to zoom noisily around the room or inspect the large worktable behind us, which is laid with coloured paper, glue, glitter pens, felt tips, shiny little coloured stars and other aids to creativity.

We begin with action songs. Tom accompanies us on the guitar, with Becky on keyboards. The children take turns to pick a song. Questions arise: What is this song telling us about God, or about Jesus? How do we pray? Modern children's songs, I notice, are much concerned with size, and animals. God is bigger than an elephant and stronger than a tiger. Who's the king of the jungle? (Answer: Jesus.) There's a good one about praying whenever I feel happy or sad, fearful or thankful. I remember, from my childhood, songs about lights ('Jesus bids us shine...') and journeys ('Michael, row the boat ashore...'). I ponder the changing priorities of Christian teaching as reflected in such songs. Is it true that there was more emphasis then on the ethical, where now prayer and propositions are in fashion? Perhaps a wider survey is required.

Tom, who is an artist, tells the story of Palm Sunday from the perspective of the foal of the ass, with the help of his own cartoon pictures. After the story, the children get down to decorating coloured paper crowns, which they are going to hang on a branch in church to celebrate Christ the King. They work together with quiet concentration, the older ones helping the younger from time to time. One or two say 'hello' to me, introducing themselves and asking my name. I tell them and they welcome me gravely. They don't seem worried by the fact that I'm a stranger. They feel safe here, and in charge. I, who so often welcome people to church, am unexpectedly moved by their welcome.

These children, only one of whom comes regularly to church on a Sunday morning, are a model Christian community—kind to each other, friendly to strangers, enthusiastic in prayer and excellent singers. When some of them come to church on special occasions, like Mothering Sunday or Easter Day, they encounter another little community, the Sunday school group. The two groups greet one another solemnly and retire to the vestry to draw pictures. I suspect that the Fun Churchers regard the Sunday Schoolers as rather deprived, as the vestry does not currently enjoy the same facilities as the village hall for handicrafts.

When good progress has been made with the crowns, there is another song, a prayer, and then jam scones and cherryade. Stephanie supervises the clearing-up. Her own daughter, she tells me, is beginning to think about applying to university. I remember when she was no older than the Fun Churchers: it seems like yesterday. Meditating unoriginally on the flight of time, I go to help Mo and Barbara wash cups and plates. Fun Church could not happen without the many members of the regular congregation who spend every other Sunday afternoon setting it up and tidying it away.

By the time we leave at five o'clock, it is dark outside and turning foggy. The brick hall looks shabby under artificial light. Railway Lane runs away into the mist—a straggle of old houses and a breaker's yard. The thickening air is stained orange and the bypass grumbles steadily under its load of traffic. The children stay close to their parents as they hurry home, still chattering cheerfully. What will they remember about Fun Church, I wonder, in 20 or 50 years' time? Impossible to tell—but surely something, and surely it will be a happy memory.

Bible Sunday

We are keeping the last Sunday of Trinity as Bible Sunday, a festival for which I have an irrational dislike. 'Isn't every Sunday a Bible Sunday?' I grumble as I labour up the hill. Isn't every *day* a Bible day? The new lectionary moves Cranmer's beautiful Collect for the second Sunday of Advent to this day:

Blessed Lord, who hast caused all holy Scriptures to be written for our learning: Grant that we may in such wise hear them, read, mark, learn, and inwardly digest them, that by patience and comfort of thy holy Word, we may embrace and ever hold fast the blessed hope of everlasting life, which thou hast given us in our Saviour Jesus Christ. Amen.

There is something profoundly moving about a human being blessing God. Usually, blessings (material or spiritual) are given by richer, wiser or more powerful beings—the ones with something to give—to their juniors or dependants. How dare we bless God? What resources do we have? One answer might be that we have love, which, as a free gift, is one of the few things we have that does not already belong to God and that God cannot demand of us. Even so, for us to bless God is like the widow giving her mite to the temple, or Abraham entertaining angels with a few hastily-made cakes. It is pure, paradoxical, holy-foolish generosity, the inestimable generosity of the inestimably poor. It is one of those touches of the sublime in humanity which hint that we are made in God's own image.

Was it reading the scriptures that caused Cranmer to bless God? Perhaps, but Cranmer doesn't insist that we all *read*: if we are illiterate, or aural-type learners, we can equally well listen. Either way, properly receiving scripture is a four-step process. Take notice of what you hear or read; learn it and absorb it; let it become part of you. This, Cranmer says, will take time. Be patient: the comfort it brings is worth the wait.

What applies to the scriptures applies also to the Prayer Book. Cranmer understood that daily prayers like Collects sink deep into our minds and colour our whole spirituality, so he gave this prayer plenty of work to do. As we say it, day after day, year after year, we notice that it is itself a microcosm of the scriptures. Beginning with the 'Blessed Lord' of the Old Testament, it takes us through to the passion of our Saviour Jesus Christ and leaves us with the hope of everlasting life. As we go on praying, we find that the Collect also mirrors the structure of Cranmer's Communion service, which begins with hearing or reading the word, digesting it and being comforted, and moves on to embrace the hope of everlasting life through the medium of bread and wine. Saying this prayer, then, becomes a way of praying the Eucharist, and the more often we say it, the more often we participate imaginatively in the Eucharist. We live, as the scriptures tell us, not by bread and wine alone but also by the word. With artful simplicity, Cranmer simultaneously reminds us to read the scriptures and immerses us more deeply in what they teach.

This thought makes me feel more positive about Bible Sunday. After lunch, prompted by the Old Testament reading ('Ho, everyone who thirsts, come to the waters...'),[27] I walk downriver under threatening skies to Sandford Lock. The willows have become sculptures of dried mud, their last leaves grey and crumbling. The river gleams like pewter. People who walk the footpath at this time of year are tranquil and self-contained. They are more likely than summer visitors to acknowledge one another as they pass, but they do not stop to talk. As I walk, I remember my favourite Collects of the Trinity season, laden as they are with memories of summer and autumn.

O God, who has prepared for them that love thee such good things as pass man's understanding: Pour into our hearts such love toward thee, that we, loving thee above all things, may obtain thy promises, which exceed all that we can desire.[28]

Let thy merciful ears, O Lord, be open to the prayers of thy humble servants; and that they may obtain their petitions make them to ask such things as shall please thee.[29]

Almighty and everlasting God, who art always more ready to hear than we to pray, and art wont to give more than either we desire or deserve: Pour down upon us the abundance of thy mercy; forgiving us those things whereof our conscience is afraid, and giving us those good things which we are not worthy to ask, but through the merits and mediation of Jesus Christ, thy Son, our Lord.[30]

Lord, we pray thee that thy grace may always prevent and follow us, and make us continually to be given to all good works.[31]

Grant, we beseech thee, merciful Lord, to thy faithful people pardon and peace; that they may be cleansed from all their sins, and serve thee with a quiet mind.[32]

Endings

I often wonder, as the liturgical year reaches another end, where we are going, if anywhere, and whether we shall know the place if we arrive. The kingdom of God is where we're going, according to tradition, but the kingdom, as Luke says, might be within us or among us, here and now. The seed of it might already have been sown; it might have been hiding beneath our feet for years.

Cycling up Rose Hill with the wind behind me, I contemplate people who cycle or drive or sail around the world. I wonder, as they finish where they began, whether they think of all those other routes they could have taken, the infinity of unexplored circumferences, and feel a sense of loss. However many times you circumnavigate the world, you won't encompass it. And if something as tangible as the globe can't be encompassed, what of human experience, where ever more paths wander through ever-expanding territories?

However we develop, there's no such thing as a completed human journey; rather, it is a lifetime's work to accept our incompleteness. Anyway, our best qualities—love, hope, creativity—are by their nature open-ended. We look forward to change, and while we're accustoming ourselves to the thought that life is incomplete, we remind ourselves that death is incomplete, too. No doubt all our energy and anticipation, all our interest in ourselves and other people, all our work and ambition come to dust and ashes, while behind us millions of people with their own energies and interests are destined for dust and ashes too. But every day we have spent on earth has had an impact and the ripples of things we have done and said widen indefinitely. We never wholly die.

Panting slightly, I reach the hilltop and check my watch (it's often later than you think). I press on past the white cherry trees, which sleep black and skeletal against the sky, their leaf-buds tightly furled and bound in bark.

John preaches on Christ the King, waking us up to the glory that is around the corner, at the beginning of Advent or at the end of time. But we are sluggish. November draws down darkness upon darkness; all we want to do is hibernate. It's almost impossible to imagine that, in a week, our blood will be quickening to cast away the works of darkness and put on the armour of light.

The round of the church year hints, as it brings us back to Advent Sunday for the tenth, or 50th, or 80th time, that whatever we're looking for is here somewhere—passed many times, perhaps; not looked for hard enough, possibly; growing among us, very probably. We don't know whether we'll ever achieve it or possess it. But if our promised end, our heaven, does not belong to us, we belong to it. It holds us in its orbit like a star.

That doesn't stop us planning for the future. Next spring, we're going to clear the weeds from the north side of the church and plant something that will look better without taking a lot of maintenance—maybe pyracantha. We're wondering whether to take out the pews and buy some chairs, to make our narrow, cell-like space more flexible. 'Change and decay in all around I see,' said Henry Lyte.[33] If he wasn't precisely wrong on both counts, I think, parking my bicycle where next year, God willing, there will be a shrubbery, it's only half the story. While we're at it, I realise, hopping round to the west door, the path could do with a load of gravel. We don't want people getting their feet soaked on the way to the Advent carol service.

The gift

God said, I bring good news
—blazoned in gold on banners of blue night
which flutter in a gale of Glorias—
who will hear it and understand?

I said, not I. Life is too short to scan
messages I could not see to read,
or fall into deep silence, sounding for
music I should lack ears to recognise.

God said, I bear a gift
here, wrapped in a cloth. Look, it is sleeping
now. Who will receive
and hold it in safe hands?

I said, not me. My hands are clawed
with grasping what they have already spoiled.
Since they tore down the apples from your tree
we have been buried deep in the cold soil.

God said, earth is renewed; journeys
begin again tonight. Are you awake?
I said, I am not ready. I am not fit.
You cannot count on weakness. Pass me by.

Said God, that other gift
you thought you had destroyed, with me is safe.
Lay down your sorrow. Let my healing kiss
burn on your lips, and come to paradise.

Notes

1   Matthew 11:3
2   Isaiah 40:3–5
3   Mark 8:35
4   1 Corinthians 12:4–7
5   Luke 1:38
6   In the English medieval carol 'I sing of a maiden'
7   T.S. Eliot, 'Journey of the Magi' (1927)
8   Matthew 16:24
9   Matthew 20:28
10 'Temptation' by Nina Cassian in *Call Yourself Alive?* translated from the Romanian by A. Deletant and B. Walker (Forest Books, 1988)
11 Psalm 139:1–2
12 Julian of Norwich, *Revelations of Divine Love* (The Long Version) 60, cf. 57–59, 61–63)
13 John 10:9 (RSV)
14 Romans 5:3–4
15 John 19:30
16 Psalm 130:1–2, 5–6
17 In the Western liturgy, the *Exultet* (so named after its first word in Latin) is the 'Paschal Proclamation', a hymn of praise sung by a deacon standing near the Paschal Candle on Holy Saturday. It dates from the seventh–eighth century.
18 Matthew 4:17, 19; 10:7–8, 25
19 Matthew 7:7
20 Luke 22:19
21 Matthew 5:43–45
22 See John 14:2 (KJV)
23 Augustine, *Confessions* 1.1
24 1 Peter 1:24 (KJV)

25 Solon of Athens, Fragment 18

26 The *Dies Irae* is part of the Mass for the Dead in the Western Church. It is thought to go back to a twelfth-century prayer of Benedictine origin.

27 Isaiah 55:1

28 Collect for the Sixth Sunday after Trinity

29 Collect for the Tenth Sunday after Trinity

30 Collect for the Twelfth Sunday after Trinity

31 Collect for the Seventeenth Sunday after Trinity

32 Collect for the Twenty-First Sunday after Trinity

33 In his famous hymn 'Abide with me'

Embracing a Concrete Desert

A spiritual journey towards wholeness

Lynne E. Chandler

'I wish I could say that I have arrived and will never have to stare into the darkness again, but I know that isn't so. I do know, though, that I have to embrace the present moment and celebrate life, whatever that may involve today. My Creator is alive within and throughout this amazing world, and has never failed to wrap me in wings of protection and comfort...'

This is the story of an unfinished journey—a journey that finds a path through struggle and difficulty to acceptance and peace of mind. It is the story of one woman choosing to seek serenity in the midst of struggles to adapt to a very different life, and discovering how, in the driest of desert places, God can reveal fresh water springs for the soul. It is a story shared through lyrical journal reflections and poems sparked by the ups and downs of life in a teeming Middle Eastern metropolis.

ISBN 978 1 84101 686 3   £5.99
Available from your local Christian bookshop or, in case of difficulty, direct from BRF using the order form on page 143.

The Road to Emmaus

Companions for the journey through life

Helen Julian CSF

This book, revised from the 2006 Lent edition, offers a chance to reflect on the experiences and teaching of seven key figures in English spirituality: Julian of Norwich, Thomas Traherne, the Venerable Bede, John Donne, John and Charles Wesley, Aelred of Rievaulx, and the anonymous author of *The Cloud of Unknowing*. We learn something of their stories, their historical context, and the themes unique to their writing.

Through the intervening centuries, their words still speak to us, illuminating truths, enriching our faith and affirming us in our own walk with God. With links to relevant Bible passages, Helen Julian suggests imaginative exercises for groups and individuals to put into practice what has been learned.

ISBN 978 1 84101 601 6   £7.99
Available from your local Christian bookshop or, in case of difficulty, direct from BRF using the order form on page 143.

Seeking Sabbath

A personal journey

David Shepherd

'How come I'm so busy I can barely catch my breath? Why do I always seem to have more work than week to do it in?' In the midst of a busy work and home routine, David Shepherd discovered that the questions he'd heard so often from others were beginning to haunt him too. In his search for answers, he came to the conclusion that something was missing— something he'd known well as a child but had since lost. Something called 'sabbath'.

Seeking Sabbath is the diary of his search for what was lost. Written over the course of six months, it draws on both his memories of peaceful childhood Sundays and the rich trove of Jewish and Christian wisdom surrounding the day of rest, without ever losing sight of the demands and realities of his present-day life. In the end, *Seeking Sabbath* is one man's attempt to rediscover a day. One week at a time.

ISBN 978 1 84101 536 1   £6.99
Available from your local Christian bookshop or, in case of difficulty, direct from BRF using the order form on page 143.

ORDERFORM

REF	TITLE	PRICE	QTY	TOTAL
686 3	Embracing a Concrete Desert	£5.99		
601 6	The Road to Emmaus	£7.99		
536 1	Seeking Sabbath	£6.99		

POSTAGE AND PACKING CHARGES				
Order value	UK	Europe	Surface	Air Mail
£7.00 & under	£1.25	£3.00	£3.50	£5.50
£7.10–£30.00	£2.25	£5.50	£6.50	£10.00
Over £30.00	FREE	prices on request		

Postage and packing	
Donation	
TOTAL	

Name _____ Account Number _____

Address _____

_____ Postcode _____

Telephone Number_____

Email _____

Payment by: ❑ Cheque ❑ Mastercard ❑ Visa ❑ Postal Order ❑ Maestro

Card no ❑❑❑❑ ❑❑❑❑ ❑❑❑❑ ❑❑❑❑ ❑❑❑

Valid from ❑❑❑❑ Expires ❑❑❑❑ Issue no. ❑❑❑

Security code* ❑❑❑ *Last 3 digits on the reverse of the card.
ESSENTIAL IN ORDER TO PROCESS YOUR ORDER   Shaded boxes for Maestro use only

Signature _____ Date _____

All orders must be accompanied by the appropriate payment.

Please send your completed order form to:
BRF, 15 The Chambers, Vineyard, Abingdon OX14 3FE
Tel. 01865 319700 / Fax. 01865 319701 Email: enquiries@brf.org.uk

❑ Please send me further information about BRF publications.

Available from your local Christian bookshop.   BRF is a Registered Charity